Saving a Life

How We Found Courage When
Death Rescued Our Son

Charles & Janet Morris

Foreword by DAN B. ALLENDER, PhD
Afterword by JONI EARECKSON TADA

Your kindness and
will always be

Saving a Life

"This is a parenting story unlike any other I've ever read…. Read until you can read no more. Don't require your heart to finish the book quickly, but promise yourself you will finish. Read and know that your suffering and the Morrises' suffering is not in vain. Redemption reigns."

—DAN B. ALLENDER, PhD,
PRESIDENT, MARS HILL GRADUATE SCHOOL

"This story of profound courage does have something we can take away. Charles and Janet 'set heart to heart' by taking us deeper into the fellowship of sharing in Christ's sufferings. And there, in the secret inner sanctum of that fellowship, they help us glimpse the source of all courage—the painfully beautiful, raw, and tender reality of our suffering Savior. He bore our hell so that one day we might have heaven. This book helped me see Jesus in that light. And that's what gives courage."

—JONI EARECKSON TADA, BEST-SELLING AUTHOR, SPEAKER

What people are saying about

SAVING A LIFE

"There may be no greater loss than the loss of a child. Charles and Janet Morris courageously share the story of their loss, but also the hope they found along the way. If you have lost a child or know someone who has, this is a 'must read' book."

—DENNIS RAINEY, PRESIDENT OF FAMILYLIFE

"*Saving a Life* is a gritty memoir about the ugliness of a child's drug addiction and the terrible beauty that comes from trusting in God, even through a parent's worst nightmare. This book certainly has the potential to be a great comfort to people in the face of horrendous pain. It hits just the right balance of tone—honesty, pain, and hope, all mixed together to create a testimony of God's redemptive work."

—GARY THOMAS, AUTHOR OF *THE BEAUTIFUL FIGHT* AND *SACRED MARRIAGE*

"*Saving a Life* has a raw, unvarnished honesty that is compelling. Just as compelling is the message of grace—grace that empowers and enables parents to hold on to God and know that He is enough. This book will enrich your love for your children and deepen your love for God and your confidence in His goodness. You will want to share this book with others."

—TEDD TRIPP, PASTOR, AUTHOR, SPEAKER

Saving a Life

How We Found Courage When
Death Rescued Our Son

Charles & Janet Morris

David C Cook®
transforming lives together

SAVING A LIFE
Published by David C. Cook
4050 Lee Vance View
Colorado Springs, CO 80918 U.S.A.

David C. Cook Distribution Canada
55 Woodslee Avenue, Paris, Ontario, Canada N3L 3E5
David C. Cook U.K., Kingsway Communications
Eastbourne, East Sussex BN23 6NT, England

LCCN 2007939846
ISBN 978-1-4347-9991-3

The Team: John Blase, Jaci Schneider, Susan Vannaman
Cover/Interior Design: The DesignWorks Group

Cover Images: ©PhotoDisc, ©iStock

Printed in the United States of America
First Edition 2008

1 2 3 4 5 6 7 8 9 10

113007

"I said to myself, 'Lo, I lie in a dream
Of separation, where there comes no sign;
My waking life is hid with Christ in God,
Where all is true and potent—fact divine.'
I will not heed the thing that doth but seem;
I will be quiet as lark upon the sod;
God's will, the seed, shall rest in me the pod."

—George MacDonald, *The Diary of an Old Soul*

CONTENTS

FOREWORD

MY SON AND I ARE IN A PERIOD of acknowledged estrangement. He is nineteen and living away from home. The conversations we have had so far are painful. He has been honest about my failures and I have had to face the effect of my life on him in new ways. At moments I have wanted desperately to defend my decisions, justify my failures as less severe than he perceives, and when explanation is not enough, I want to quit. The urge to quit—to throw my hands in the air and say, "Fine, you want to go your way—do it on your own penny"—is greater at moments than my faith and patience. I haven't quit; I haven't justified my failures (too often). And my son has spoken more clearly and passionately to me than he has in years. We are both hopeful, yet the process of growth together in Christ stretches out over many mountain passes, and the inn where I so desperately desire to lay my head is not yet in sight.

It is in that season that I read this demanding book. Some days I could not pick up the pages of the manuscript. The pain of the Morrises was too raw and it seemed to send a surge of agony through my body like sciatica. In those times I could not read, but I also could not forget. I found myself saying, "How could you let such good and loving parents suffer such loss?"

I ached for them, but in fact, I was at war with myself, and even more, I was in a pitched battle with God.

The central question I struggled to answer was this: Could I love and serve a God who allowed my son to die? Could I trust and surrender to a God who might allow my son to turn from me and from Him? The pain of a heartbroken parent is a wail that is deeper than any I have heard on this earth. What would I do with my own heartache? What would I do with the heartache that I had not yet suffered, but as any parent, I know I might?

I finished the book. I can tell you I am immensely heartened for the hard journey. I promise there are no easy answers in this glorious labor of love. The Morrises do not trivialize their son's death, or the death and resurrection of Jesus, by offering clichéd hope. What they offer, and far more live, with integrity is the promise that those who mourn will be comforted. How? When? I don't know. I simply believe and can say: "I, too, have known the kindness of God in the midst of my turning to him and away from the natural call to fury or indifference."

This is a parenting story unlike any other I've ever read. It is raw, real, and alive with the promise that there is no condemnation for those who are in Christ Jesus. Every parent fails. Christian parents seem to fail in even greater ways given our desire to offer a profound picture of the love of God for our children. If we do not enter His deep, abiding passion of delight for us as parents, we can never offer the hope of forgiveness for our children. For many of us it means surrendering our fears, demands, and self-righteousness. For others it may involve surrendering our self-reproach and regret. What does it mean for us to throw ourselves on the mercy of Jesus and then to rise dancing before those who see us as foolish and broken? This book will take you by the hand and lead you through death without letting you forget the rising hope of redemption. The Morrises will allow you to see how wailing can lead to laughter and how despair can be transformed into hope.

One last bit of counsel—read until you can read no more. Don't require your heart to finish the book quickly, but promise yourself you will finish. Read and know that your suffering and the Morrises' suffering is not in vain. Redemption reigns.

—Dan B. Allender, PhD
president of Mars Hill Graduate School
author of *To Be Told* and *Leading with a Limp*

August 5, 2003

Friends,

You may have heard by now, but I'm sending an e-mail blast to everyone in this address book.

Our son, Jeff, would have been 23 today, but the Lord took him home last Saturday. It will be weeks before we know the exact cause of death, but it looks fairly certain that he died of a drug overdose.

His body is being flown back to Oklahoma, and we leave tomorrow afternoon with our son, Peter, for a Friday service. Our daughter, Katie, and her husband, Richard, are driving there now from Washington with our two grandchildren.

We are in great sorrow. We wept through church on Sunday morning as the gospel was proclaimed. Our son suffered his entire life from depression. In his teens he started sampling a variety of drugs and from then on his life was up and down.

We tried everything we humanly knew, and each step was spent in considerable time on our knees, pleading with the Lord to grant a breakthrough.

Janet and I are convinced that the Lord has broken through at last and taken Jeff to be with Him in glory.

In Christ,
Charles Morris

PREFACE

THIS IS THE STORY OF A YOUNG MAN, the son of Christian parents, found dead on a bathroom floor from an overdose of methamphetamine. His name was Jeff. It's the story told by his parents as we experienced it—Janet tells the story, but she speaks for both of us. We've tried to tell it as sincerely as we could, without any filters, without playing to any audiences. His death left us raw with pain and desperate like the psalmist, crying out to God for comfort and for something more solid than comfort—something like courage.

We've tried to communicate not only the comfort but also the courage that God communicated to us, right at the point of our need, and to do it with the same power and deep conviction he used in speaking it to us. We've done it with the hope that the Lord will use our words to pour courage into your heart.

This is certainly not a book about how to succeed at the job of parenting. If the performance review for parents is the grown-up child—how he turns out—then this book is about utter parenting failure and we honestly have no advice for anyone on how to avoid it. If we started trying to analyze where we went wrong, or what we'd do differently in retrospect, the real issue would get lost—the real issue is not what we have done or failed to do but what God has done for us through Jesus Christ, for all of us who believe in him.

If you want a summary of our parenting efforts, read Isaiah 26:18 (NASB):

> We were pregnant, we writhed
> in labor,
> We gave birth, as it seems, only
> to wind.
> We could not accomplish deliv-
> erance for the earth.
> Nor were inhabitants of the
> world born.

These are the brokenhearted words of parents whose efforts to give birth failed. Isaiah isn't talking about the labor to give birth to natural-born children. He's talking about spiritually born children, sons and daughters who will truly live, and these words are a lament over how we try and fail to accomplish that rebirth: "We couldn't deliver. We tried, but all our efforts were in vain."

But right at that point, that point of failure, the Lord enters the picture. The next words are charged with hope: "Your dead will live! Their corpses will rise!" (26:19). In other words, "I, God, will do what you couldn't do!" That's the point, not only of our story, of our experience, but of the entire human race.

The Son of God has entered the picture and has done what we could not do for ourselves.

Grace is the hardest thing for us to grasp—grace, pure and simple, stripped of all the mitigating circumstances, completely outrageous. Grace says that Jesus has done the whole deal. It's meant to be drunk straight and undiluted. It's meant to be believed in full view of all our failure, sin, and weakness, right in the face of that which appears to defy it, because God has told us that it's true. Grace is meant to set us free to rejoice in our God. God told those parents, "You who lie in the dust, awake and shout for joy" (26:19). Wake up out of discouragement and fear and grief. Wake up and shake off every shred of condemnation and hopelessness. Throw your lives on the altar because Jesus has done what you couldn't do.

We have three beloved children but this is the story of our middle child, Jeff. His story is a brazen picture of God's grace and we want to tell it in hopes that the grace of God will come through loud and clear, without interference. If you can identify with us and if you can identify with Jeff, then the grace of God is going to be the best news you ever heard—too good to be true, yet true nonetheless—and the source of all our courage.

It really boils down to this—it's not about us, it's all about Jesus. That's courage—in a nutshell.

—Charles and Janet Morris

1

Finding
Courage ...

when the
blow falls

WORDS BRING US OUR NEWS—our worst news and our best news.

Charles and I were sitting in the living room with the windows wide open to the afternoon sea breeze, talking about something, I don't remember what, when the phone rang. It didn't set off any particular alarms in us. I answered it, as unsuspecting as anyone in these situations, but in one instant and a few words, everything changed.

Jeff's girlfriend, Suzanne, was on the line, wailing incoherently, and I responded by clicking into calm-and-under-control mode. "Take a deep breath, honey, and say that again." Whatever it was, we would absorb the shock and deal with it, as we'd been dealing with crises in Jeff's life for years.

"Oh Janet, Jeff's dead. He's dead."

"Suzanne, that's not possible."

That's what I said and that's what I meant. In my mind there was no place for that possibility. Jeff could not be dead. Not that he hadn't come close plenty of times, with two suicide attempts and years of drug use and addiction. He'd been careening near the edge for a long time.

Parents hope all things, but we were veterans, and in spite of the latest six months of rehab, we hadn't breathed any sighs of relief. Addiction is vicious, and Jeff's bright and beautiful mind seemed damaged from his years of use—especially after his graduation to speed. His drug of choice had been "whatever." But when he started using speed, he began to change, to lapse into paranoid delusions, which were terrifying for him and for us.

Even after months of sobriety, he still wasn't thinking straight or reacting normally. He had this little hesitation before he answered questions, as if he had to pull himself back from wherever he was. Sometimes you'd catch him pacing around muttering in a cognitive world of his own. So we were still on alert, still braced.

Too many times we'd thought, "This time he'll get past it," only to watch everything collapse yet again. Rehab, medication, counseling. We had hopefully, urgently, sought out one solution after another. At that point it would have been naïve to have optimistic expectations based on what we saw in Jeff or what one more program might do for him. But we were looking past all of that to Jesus. We didn't have any clear picture in our mind of what we expected from Him, but we knew He'd heard our prayers and that He was able and willing to save our son. We had peace about it. Some intervention, some work of power and grace would come from the Lord and blow the little flickering flame of Jeff's faith into a blaze that would set him free. This was why those words, "Jeff is dead," were impossible.

Impossible, but true.

Turning onto Jeff's street in San Clemente thirty minutes later, we saw police cars lining the sidewalk, three of them, with lights flashing. I glanced up to his second-floor apartment and saw his bike chained to the rail of his balcony. Behind that balcony my son's body lay, dead on the bathroom floor where Suzanne had found him. Unbelievable.

My mind raced to get up there and see him, do something, get some answers, but my body moved in slow motion as we stepped out of the car. Somehow my legs carried me dazedly in the direction of the stairs to his apartment. A policeman took charge of us after first determining we weren't just mildly curious onlookers stopping to ask questions. We were VIPs, parents of the victim. Pulling us aside, he gave us our first little bits of information. I stared at the yellow crime-scene tape blocking the stairway and listened to him explain that we weren't allowed up because an investigation was underway. They had seen no signs of foul play, nor found a suicide note, and that's all they knew so far. Soon the coroner would arrive and remove the body, and in the meantime a neighbor had opened her apartment downstairs where I could hear Suzanne sobbing. I went in, hugged her, came out and sat on the step with our eighteen-year-old son, Peter. I was introverting, desperately wishing I could be alone to think and pray.

Charles, the extrovert, was talking to people. Eventually he brought two officers over to introduce them, explaining that they were chaplains, routinely dispatched in these situations to minister to family and friends of the victim. But they were more than that; they were believers. For Charles, the presence of those men was like Jesus arriving on the scene of our nightmare and turning it into a place of worship and witness. It quickly came out that Charles and I were also believers, and that he was the speaker on a Christian radio program, *Haven Today*. From then on, as he said later, "It was a camp meeting of faith." Instantly bonding with Charles in the knowledge of Jesus, they freely shared the gospel with Suzanne and much later, after the coroner's van drove away, joined us in a circle in Jeff's apartment and conducted a little worship service.

But that was Charles. To me it all skimmed over the surface. Underneath, I was in free fall. Something was collapsing inside me and I had to get away and figure it out. I had this clammy fear about letting Peter out of my sight, so I asked him to walk down to the beach with me instead of doing what he wanted to do, which was call his friends and get away.

When we got there, the pain and something like fear intensified into a crisis. The juncture of all those young people enjoying a carefree San Clemente day at the beach and my son's body laying two blocks away made my knees buckle with every step. It was that old familiar pain of Jeff's exclusion from the normal good-ness of life. Only now he was finally, fatally excluded. It combined with the anguish of having trusted in the Lord for a rescue, an intervention, that hadn't come. A great silent wave of grief was welling up inside of me but this loss of certainty about the Lord was even more terrifying.

I mouthed out a desperate cry, "Jesus! Help me!" In my hand I was clutching a purse-sized Bible. I didn't know what to look for; I only knew I was desperate to hear something from Jesus, so I stood still and opened it. The crowd streamed past us, the surfers calling it a day in the fading pink light, and the book's pages whipped around in the wind. I held them down with my thumbs and brought the words up close and read Hebrews 10:17 (NASB):

> Their sins and their lawless
> deeds I will remember no more.

As I read those words, they came to me like light reaching into darkness, like landing on solid ground. Those words changed everything. Jesus was making a declaration, bringing down his gavel like a judge announcing a final, favorable ruling concerning our son. It became clear to me as I stood there on the beach and read those words that Jeff's well-being was firmly established in the heavenly realm. In defiance of his death, Jesus presented this reality to me to believe. It didn't matter what his status appeared to be in the context of that San Clemente beach. It didn't ultimately matter that we hadn't seen him transformed in the "land of the living" as the Bible calls it. What mattered was his standing in the sight of God. His whole life depended on that verdict.

Bang, the gavel of His justice fell and the judge rendered the blood-bought judgment, "His sins are forgiven and his lawless deeds remembered no more." It rang out into the early evening air with the weight of ultimate authority—the same authority that said, "Let there be light," and there was light. Those words declared Jeff's ultimate and complete well-being. They were what Jesus went to the depths to accomplish, and like a champion victorious from battle, He was declaring the prize He'd won through death, the key to unseen realms of glory, and He was telling me to listen: This is the verdict. His sins and lawless deeds are remembered no more. They have been removed.

So Jesus had not arrived too late after all. The rescue had come two thousand years ago on the cross.

"Your prayers have been heard! All is well!" That was the message on the beach that night. The details of the "all" weren't completely clear but the Lord disclosed them to us in wondrous ways over the days and weeks to come. And taught us a great deal about courage.

Finding Courage ...
in their words:

Dear Haven,

I try to listen to your program every morning. I was especially touched by Charles Morris' story about his son's death. I am praying for his family. If he has time to read this I would like to send him some words of encouragement. I have three sons and my middle son was killed in a motorcycle accident a few days before his 24th birthday.

Hearing him talk reminded me of the first few days after my son's death—it was like a fog and yet the pain was very sharp. I know now that our dear Lord was sheltering me from much of the pain with His loving arms. My heart was broken and my world was shattered.

When I first heard my news I begged God to not let it be so—let there be a way out of this and he be alive. I was frantic with disbelief. But God very clearly spoke to my heart that it was true and that it had to be this way and that I just had to trust Him for the reasons. He reminded me that He had recently allowed me to confirm my son's salvation at a wonderful dinner we had together. I knew I had to dwell on that for that was the eternal. This life is only temporary—for all of us.

I believe I will understand it all when I get to Glory but for now I just need to trust His loving heart. He has proven His love to me in so many ways throughout my life.

In Him,

Tim

୬

Dearest Charles & Janet Morris,

I am writing to offer my sincere condolences for your dear son. I am so sorry. My heart goes out to you because I have a son that is 18 years old that struggles with life. I'm in constant prayer for my son and all I can do is lift him up daily. Here are some words from our Lord that I pray will encourage you:

"Who shall separate us from the love of Christ? Shall trouble or hardship or persecution or famine or nakedness or danger or sword?... No, in all these things we are more than conquerors through him who loved us" Rom. 8:35, 37.

"The Spirit of the Sovereign Lord is on me, because the Lord has anointed me to ... provide for those who grieve in Zion—to bestow on them a crown of beauty instead of ashes, the oil of gladness instead of mourning, and a garment of praise instead of a spirit of despair" Is. 61:1.

"You will grieve, but your grief will turn to joy.... Now is your time of grief, but I will see you again and you will rejoice, and no one will take away your joy" John 16:20, 22.

"You hear, O Lord, the desire of the afflicted; you encourage them, and you listen to their cry" Psalm 10:17.

Your family will be in my prayers and thoughts.

God Bless you,

Denise

Finding Courage ...
in the Word:

ISAIAH 44:21–22

*I will not forget you. I have swept away your offenses like a cloud,
your sins like the morning mist.*

ISAIAH 51:22

*See, I have taken out of your hand the cup that made you stag-
ger; from that cup, the goblet of my wrath, you will never drink
again.*

MATTHEW 1:21

*You are to give him the name Jesus, because he will save his people
from their sins.*

ROMANS 4:7–8

*Blessed are they whose transgressions are forgiven, whose sins are cov-
ered. Blessed is the man whose sin the Lord will never count against
him.*

EPHESIANS 1:7

*In him we have redemption through his blood, the forgiveness of sins,
in accordance with the riches of God's grace.*

COLOSSIANS 2:13–14

*He forgave us all our sins, having canceled the written code, with
its regulations, that was against us and that stood opposed to us;
he took it away, nailing it to the cross.*

HEBREWS 10:17

Their sins and lawless acts I will remember no more.

2

Finding
Courage ...

in a sign

BEING JEFF'S PARENTS MEANT BEING in a constant state of emergency. The red lights on the control panel never stopped flashing. We were continually, urgently searching for the place where he would fit, where he would belong and begin to thrive.

At age two he seemed delightfully quirky and imaginative, always improvising costumes and doing unexpected things. Like in Busy Bee Preschool, when it was his turn at the easel with the tempera paints. Miss Mary smocked him up and left him, brush in hand. A few minutes later she came back to find the big sheet of white paper untouched and Jeff's blond hair painted completely green.

She suggested that maybe preschool wasn't the place for him just yet. Eventually we got used to hearing that kind of thing. In every situation problems and concerns eventually emerged:

"Perhaps Jeff needs to be in a less structured environment."

"Maybe a Little League team with younger kids."

"He's just too fidgety and easily distracted to be in the boys choir."

"Small for his age. Getting bullied. In his own world."

I remember overhearing a teacher describe him as "the one who scowls all the time." I cried and then said to him, "Honey, try to smile more."

Jeff was the one who fell through the ice on the pond, who ran out in the street and got hit by a car when all the other kids stopped at the curb. He was the one who was almost abducted by a stranger at the Disneyland hotel, who got on elevators and disappeared as his grandparents stood helplessly watching the lights signal a stop at every floor. He went through life like somebody's target.

It seemed that even his soul was vulnerable. Walking into kindergarten class the first day, his scrunched-up body language broadcast to the world that he was painfully self-conscious. His collars would be chewed at the end of a day. The teacher said they called him "the billy goat" because he ate everything from pencils to glue. He mangled his work papers, covering them with doodles. He never seemed to know what he was supposed to be doing—if everyone else was lined up to go out to recess, he was still at his desk. If everyone else turned left, he turned right, oblivious to the world around him half the time.

At first the kids laughed at him. When it was my turn to bring the class snack, I would bleed for him; he so obviously wasn't a part of things. Eventually he learned to get laughs on purpose and find a place on the fringe. But he didn't have any sense of boundaries. He was a great wit, a reader, writer, artist, and yet he always pushed to the edge—the edge of the truth, of what he could safely handle, of what he could get away with.

Finally, at a parent-teacher conference, his fourth-grade teacher at his Christian school told us, gently but firmly, "Jeff isn't functioning well. He doesn't fit in. He needs more individual attention than I can give him. This isn't the place for him. You need to have him tested and find out what's going on."

That's when we really went into gear. In Bret Lott's novel *Jewel*, the mother gives birth to a Down Syndrome little girl, and from then on, her life is mobilized to find help for her child. "We're saving a life here," she would say. I think that's what happened with us after that conference—we went into lifesaving mode.

The first thing we did was take him to Philadelphia, to Bryn Mawr College, where they put him through a three-day marathon of diagnostic tests while we took turns entertaining Peter in the waiting room, pulling snacks and toys out of the travel bag, and taking him for walks around the campus. Finally they summoned us for the diagnosis, which boiled down to this: "Very bright but with severe attention-related learning disabilities and extremely low self-esteem."

Their recommendation was that we find a "multisensory learning environment."

Okay. We're saving a life here. Try as we might, we couldn't find that kind of "learning environment" in Florida, so we packed up the family, moved to Colorado, and enrolled all the kids in a private school. It boasted a hands-on, loosely structured, individualized class-room setting with a we-won't-make-anyone-feel-bad approach to student evaluation. Maybe this was it. Maybe we'd found the right "pond" for our fish to swim in. Maybe his self-esteem would begin to take an upward turn and his future would brighten as he found his stride.

It was not to be.

In eighth grade he was kicked out for buying marijuana from a schoolmate. Soon he was in a cycle of heavy marijuana use and depression, and it just kept getting worse. We went from context to context—home school, public school, Christian school—and when-ever things went wrong, we tried to clean the slate and find a fresh place for him to start again. Every time it was like Noah after the flood. The world might have been clean and sparkling with promise, but before you knew it, Noah was drunk. Counselors, rehabs, noth-ing worked; things just kept spiraling more out of control.

What was going on behind those blue eyes? What fears did he have? Why did he take that first little baggie of marijuana and go off into Bear Creek Park and figure out how to roll it into a joint? What was he thinking? We don't know. We don't even know if it was the first time. Was he "self-medicating" his anxiety and depression like so many experts told us? Why did he seem fascinated with anything for-bidden, drawn to anything dangerous? Was it because the "normal world" was always out of his comfort zone so he tried to find another place to be? Were they simply choices, sinful choices, he made?

And why didn't his faith help him more? All we knew was that he was in danger and we couldn't save him and he couldn't save himself. Only the Lord could save him. While we did what we could on a practical level, we were looking to the Lord for help, and even in our alarm, a "yes" seemed to come to us from the Lord when we prayed—a "yes" that calmed our fears.

One Sunday afternoon after church several years ago, I was driving up the eight-mile dirt road to our mountaintop home in Colorado. "Drive" doesn't quite do it justice. In eight miles and twenty-one switchbacks, the road climbed two thousand feet in elevation. Our home was a beautiful set-apart place and, we hoped, remote enough to put trouble and Jeff at a safe distance from each other.

We'd taken three cars to church that morning. Charles was staying after for an elders meeting, Peter had gone home with a friend, our daughter Kate was already away at college, and Jeff, with a new driver's license, had dashed away after Sunday school in our little old Nova. I drove the third car home.

It was one of those days when our hopes for Jeff were crumbling away again. We had been hopeful. His involvement in youth group, his love for the Lord and interest in the Scriptures had all been greatly encouraging—and then everything seemed to come apart with the advent of a new friendship. Dan was pierced and spiked and disaffected from life, and while we watched them bond like kindred spirits, our hearts went heavy with dread.

I drove up the road worrying, "the problem of Jeff" going around and around in my head. Suddenly the Nova went barreling by me, heading back down the road. As he passed, I caught a quick glimpse of Jeff's face. The words that came to mind were "hell-bent." He was almost certainly on his way to no good and my panic amplified a few notches.

I cried out loud: "Lord, there he goes. What will save him?"

A few switchbacks later I had to stop because a man was standing in the road, his car pulled over with the engine still running. Up ahead a few yards stood a bighorn sheep, perfectly still, with his big ribbed horns curving back in a semicircle. He looked patient and majestic standing there in the dappled light, allowing us to get a good long look at him before he crashed away into the thicket.

"I've lived here twenty-one years and I've never seen a bighorn sheep on this mountain," the man said. "And did you notice? It was a male, and they're really rare."

Was it a sign? We come from the Christian camp that doesn't look for signs and basically doesn't trust them. The mode of thinking is: If you search for answers outside God's Word, you're opening yourself up for who knows what.

But this sign—this ram in the road—it *pointed* to the Word of God. It pointed straight to the story of Abraham and Isaac and to the ram God gave as a substitute.

God told Abraham to take his son, Isaac, up the mountain and to offer him as a sacrifice, and Abraham wasted no time obeying. As they were on their way up, Isaac asked, "I see the fire and the wood, but where's the lamb for the burnt offering?" The son didn't realize the import of his question but the father certainly did. Where was the substitute for Isaac? How would he be saved? Who would take his place on the altar?

Abraham told Isaac, "God will provide." And God did. Just as Abraham was about to sacrifice Isaac, God stopped him and Abraham saw a ram caught by his horns in the thicket. He sacrificed it in Isaac's place.

That ram, provided by God, saved the son's life and secured the father's future. It was a sign pointing to the true Ram—the ultimate substitute provided by God when He gave His own Son to die.

It seemed to us the Lord was showing us where to hang our hopes for Jeff. He was fixing our eyes on the Ram—Jesus—and to the great promise contained in what Jesus did as the substitute. The answer to my question, "What will save him?" was, "Look! This is what saves sons! Stop looking at the problems. Look at the ram and take hope."

We held tightly to that hope thinking it meant an intervention, a deliverance, a great transformation.

Death came instead and seemed to mock our hopes.

We needed to have the other word, the word of life, trumpet its courage into us again and again in the face of this incontrovertible fact of Jeff's death.

The day after his death was a Sunday, for which we were very thankful. We felt drawn to church by our great need for the Lord and for the comforting company of believers. As we took our places, one of the elders, Herb, turned around and hugged us and prayed with us and then later walked up to the pulpit and prayed for us again. His wife, Debby, had tears of sympathy running down her face nonstop during the service. The pastor, Ted, and his wife, Linda, are two of the most rare and precious friends you'll ever find. They'd both been with us the night before, staying into the wee hours of the morning.

Ted preached Christ that morning with a kind of raw impassioned conviction. Then came the baskets of bread and the little cups of wine passing from one to another—His body broken, His blood shed—the objective guarantee of the "all is well." I don't think I ever partook of the bread and wine with a more intentional gratitude or with a clearer-eyed grasp of what they meant.

Then we sang a song—one that was new to us. The words were courage-charged. They were bold words claiming a great justification in the face of great sin. If sung presumptuously to excuse sin, they would have been blasphemous. But sung as words of faith, they belied sin and sorrow and death. In the face of it all, they declared Jesus as the guarantee of our place before the throne of God. No one can kick us out, no one can tell us we don't belong.

Before the throne of God above
I have a strong and perfect plea
A great high Priest whose name is Love
Who ever lives and pleads for me.
My name is graven on his hands,

My name is written on his heart.
I know that while in heaven he stands
No tongue can bid me thence depart.

When Satan tempts me to despair
And tells me of the guilt within,
Upward I look and see him there
Who made an end of all my sin.
Because the sinless Savior died
My sinful soul is counted free,
For God the just is satisfied
To look on him and pardon me.

Behold him there the risen Lamb
My perfect spotless righteousness
The great unchangeable I AM
King of glory and of grace.
One with himself I cannot die.
My soul is purchased by his blood,
My life is hid with Christ on high,
With Christ my Savior and my God.

As we sang it, the "yes" was resounding in our hearts. Yes! This is reality. Jesus is salvation. These words are true for us and for our son. His place before the throne of God is secure, his sins and lawless deeds are remembered no more, and he is safely home.

As we drove home, we talked on the cell phone with our daughter, Kate. She lives in eastern Washington with her husband, Richard, who is a pastor, and their two adorable little girls, Charlotte and Grace. We'd talked with Kate as we raced to the apartment, giving her the news as it broke. Now we were telling her how heartbreaking and yet joyous church had been for us. Before we mentioned the song, she said, "It was that way for me, too. I cried through the whole thing but at the same time I was just full of joy. Richard picked this song earlier in the week that I'd never heard before. It was amazing what I felt as we sang it—about myself—but also about Jeff; how he's okay right now because of Jesus."

"What was the song?" I asked her.

"It's called 'Before the Throne of God Above.'"

We were awed by the confirmation of this little "coincidence." For years our love for Jeff had revved up our advocacy for him, driving us to find answers for him and yet, as fueled as it had been, our advocacy had failed. But Jesus—the Great I AM whose name is "Love"—this Jesus had taken up Jeff's cause and, unlike ours, his advocacy had not failed. The gladness of that realization is beyond anything words can express.

When Abraham prayed for Ishmael, he asked just one thing, "If only he could dwell in your presence." God said, "No," and then offered Abraham a consolation prize for Ishmael. "Look, I will bless him, and will make him fruitful and will multiply him exceedingly. He shall become the father of twelve princes, and I will make him a great nation."

It sounds like the jackpot but in reality it was Isaac, the son of the promise, who got the real prize. He wasn't sent away. He dwelt in the presence of God. As contrary to appearances as it might be, we believed the answer to all our prayers for Jeff was a resounding "Yes!" He is an Isaac. He is in God's presence and no one can "bid him thence depart." Thanks to Jesus, no one can say to him, "Get out, you don't belong here."

Finding Courage ...
in their words:

Dear Charles and Janet,

Bob forwarded your letter to me about Jeff.
Words cannot tell you about the sorrow of my heart
as I read the news. Janet, remember the Ram that
you met on the road in Colorado? I have often
thought of that story and told it many times. There
was a substitute for Isaac, and for Jeff. May His
arms enfold you during this most difficult time of
your life.

All my love and prayers.

Rose Marie

Good Morning Charles,

I heard you on the radio sharing your loss
with your family-through-the radio. I am not
much of an encourager, but, when I heard you that
evening while I was driving, I felt your pain and
I felt the importance that you (and others that
God uses) are to sinners like us. Three years ago, I
was going through a depression and many nights
your comforting words calmed me and put me to
sleep feeling safe in the Lord. Before listening to

you, I would spend many, many nights awake in fear trembling and crying with my heart filled with fear, guilt & hurt.

I gave my life to God while listening to you.

That evening you shared your words of loss and I felt the pain in your voice, but yet there was something so profound in your voice that I cannot explain. It was like I felt your open wound or your faith in the raw ... Like it was all you had, your faith.......

I was so overwhelmed with your courage and it just showed me your true loyalty to God. I felt the need to thank you for the many nights your voice was the only comfort to my heart, the voice that God uses to comfort many like me.

Your message that evening also awakened the revealing fact that we are a family of God through the radio.

Jim

Dear Janet and Charles,

Your heartbreaking message came and we wept with you and your family over the loss of Jeff. I cannot fully enter your loss and grief, no one can who has not undergone the same tragedy. But Jesus has and does enter this with you both, with you all.

I hope this note will be another small reminder of the unbreakable bonds that exist between all of us who are together "in Christ." Indeed, death itself cannot break these bonds between us and those who, like your beloved son, Jeff, are among "the dead in Christ."

I rejoice over every memory of our past times together and join with K in sending our love, sympathy, and best wishes to you for greater service and usefulness in the work of the glorious Gospel of Grace.

Thom and Kathy

~

Dear Charles, Janet, and Peter,

Bonnie and I, along with our family and church, have been grieving over the loss of your son, Jeffrey. I listened to the broadcast. Well done, my friend. Katie spoke so tenderly. It was medicine to my own heart as, in the Spirit, I suffered with you.

C. S. Lewis once wrote, "Human death is the result of sin and the triumph of Satan. But it is also the means of redemption from sin, God's medicine for man and his weapon against Satan."

May what has happened have been the weapon God used to rescue one of His little sheep from the teeth of the Wolf.

May God's grace carry you through the days ahead, as you trust in Him. Please give each other a big hug from us,

Love in the Lord,

Mart

Finding Courage ...
in the Word:

GENESIS 22:7–8

Isaac spoke up and said to his father Abraham, "'Father." "Yes, my son?" Abraham replied. "The fire and wood are here," Isaac said, "but where is the lamb for the burnt offering?" Abraham answered, "God himself will provide the lamb for the burnt offering, my son."

GENESIS 22:14

So Abraham called that place "The LORD Will Provide." And to this day it is said, "On the mountain of the LORD it will be provided."

PSALM 5:7

I, by your great mercy, will come into your house; in reverence will I bow down toward your holy temple.

ISAIAH 50:7–8

I will not be put to shame. He who vindicates me is near. Who then will bring charges against me?

ISAIAH 53:6–7

We all, like sheep, have gone astray, each of us has turned to his own way; and the LORD has laid on him the iniquity of us all. He was oppressed and afflicted, yet he did not open his mouth; he was led like a lamb to the slaughter, and as a sheep before her shearers is silent, so he did not open his mouth.

ISAIAH 54:17

"No weapon forged against you will prevail, and you will refute every tongue that accuses you. This is the heritage of the servants of the LORD, and this is their vindication from me," declares the LORD.

ROMANS 3:25

> *God presented him as a sacrifice of atonement, through faith in his blood."*

ROMANS 8:33–34

> *Who will bring any charge against those whom God has chosen? It is God who justifies. Who is he that condemns? Christ Jesus, who died—more than that, who was raised to life—is at the right hand of God and is also interceding for us.*

GALATIANS 4:28

> *Now you, brothers, like Isaac, are children of promise."*

HEBREWS 10:19–22

> *Therefore, brothers, since we have confidence to enter the Most Holy Place by the blood of Jesus, by a new and living way opened for us through the curtain, that is, his body, and since we have a great priest over the house of God, let us draw near to God with a sincere heart in full assurance of faith.*

1 PETER 1:18

> *For you know that it was not with perishable things such as silver or gold that you were redeemed from the empty way of life handed down to you from your forefathers, but with the precious blood of Christ, a lamb without blemish or defect.*

3

Finding
Courage ...

in a
children's tale

ON THE COFFEE TABLE LAY A COPY OF *The Silver Chair* by C. S. Lewis, one of his Narnia tales for children. It had been there since before the call from Suzanne, returned by one of Peter's friends who'd borrowed it, and it remained on the table, waiting to tell us something.

We were in sore need of hearing something. Here it was only Sunday evening and already the joy we'd experienced in church had ebbed away as the fact of Jeff's death rolled over us again like fresh news. An autopsy that didn't bear thinking about had taken place, and the coroner called late in the day. It still looked like a drug overdose but the laboratory results wouldn't be back for some time—weeks.

Neither of us put it into words, but unformed questions were nagging at our hearts, disturbing the waters—questions about Jeff's faith. Who was Jeff? Was he a believer? His true identity seemed impossible to define because he was like two people.

Three months earlier he'd been facing the very real possibility of doing jail time for his DUIs. He was terrified of being behind bars. "I know what it's like Mom, I know plenty of guys from AA who've been there, and I don't want to tell you about it because it would upset you too much."

But then he'd tell me—how the newcomer to jail was always challenged and intimidated and how if you showed any fear you were finished. And the guards, he was sure, were just as bad. You were trapped in a place where there was no mercy, no safety unless you proved yourself merciless. He was steeling himself to be cocky, unafraid, and bad enough to survive. Our words were wasted; we were naïve, sheltered. Jail was a world beyond our protection, and he was hardening himself to face it alone.

Then other times his faith would emerge. Like the afternoon we were walking up and down the grocery aisles, picking out what he wanted to eat during a Sunday afternoon visit to our house. He'd expected to hear back from his lawyer about the negotiations to get him house arrest instead of jail, but the lawyer hadn't returned any of his calls and time had almost run out.

"Mom, I've been thinking about what First Peter says about how we shouldn't suffer for doing something bad but if we suffer for Jesus, we should be glad. I'm going to jail for something bad, but it can turn into something good if I go in as a Christian and witness for Jesus. Then whatever happens to me—even if I die or walk out with scars—it'll be good, it'll be for Jesus."

A few days later his lawyer called and told him the house arrest was on—no jail—but went on to say it was more than he deserved, he was just a punk kid, and next time he wouldn't be able to do anything for him. Jeff was crushed, diminished like a little boy, and then angry. Very angry. Those "whatever happens to me ... it'll be for Jesus" thoughts quickly disappeared as he plotted how to make the most of his new lease on life. We saw the hard, closed look on his face and knew he'd retreated into a bad place. We didn't know if it was a delusional world of his damaged mind or the orphan world of his unbelief.

The Sunday before he died, he came over, and he was the old sweet Jeff again. He'd decided to move out of his living arrangement with Suzanne because he knew it "wasn't good with Jesus," but he didn't know where to go next. Coming home was not an option, but we offered to help him find a place close by.

We told him, "You need to rebuild your life in the company of believers; people who can come around you and build up your faith."

He called us after he got home that night and said, "I just want you to know I heard you today." There was that undefensive quality to his voice—a repentance, a softening to the Lord.

Later we found out he tried to reach a Christian friend the Monday before he died but couldn't get through. He was fired from his Subway job on Tuesday for not showing up the

Saturday before, when the processing for his house arrest had taken longer than expected. Friday, the day before he died, they came and put the electronic "shackles" on to monitor his enforced confinement. He wouldn't be allowed to leave the apartment for two months except to go to work—to a job he no longer had. That night he called his dealer and bought a huge supply of methamphetamine and that's how he overdosed—alone in the bathroom, apparently by accident. His tolerance was low because he hadn't used in so long. Or maybe he just wanted to go out with a bang.

We didn't have all that information as we sat there that evening, drained and hurting. All we knew was that we were never sure which Jeff was going to show up next. When he was using, it was the worst. Anyone who's lived with an addict knows how every resource is harnessed for one all-consuming agenda—get the drug. Life becomes a single self-serving effort to stay supplied. Manipulation, blame, deceit, stealing, you name it; it's part of the repertoire, and if the supply is threatened, anger erupts.

When he was sober, another person would emerge. Sweet, loving Jesus, but very vulnerable and never really free. Who was the real Jeff? What about his faith in Jesus? Was it enough?

As we thought about Jeff, our courage ebbed away. *The Silver Chair,* lying there on the table, was like a phone with its message light blinking. Eventually it attracted our notice; we remembered the story we'd read years ago to the kids, and then—zap!—suddenly we were galvanized with a metaphor for understanding Jeff's life and death.

It's the story of Prince Rilian. He goes out to avenge the death of his mother, but an evil queen seduces him and lures him into her underground realm. Most of the time he's completely deluded and believes everything the queen tells him, all her flattery and her spin on reality. But for a few moments every day, he returns to sanity. He sees the situation for what it is, he remembers his true identity and resists the queen and her enchantment. And yet, all his efforts are useless because during those lucid episodes the queen always chains him to a chair. Try as he might, he can't break the chains. All he can do is struggle and desperately cry out for help in the name of Aslan, the great Lion, the Lord of Narnia, Lewis's Christ figure.

The point of the book is that Aslan responds to the prince's cry. He sends a rescue party made up of two children (Jill and Eustace) and a Marshwiggle (Puddleglum). After several foolish diversions they arrive on the scene and set him free. The spell is broken and Rilian returns to the sunlit lands, sane and in his right mind, free at last from the unwholesome delusion that held him captive for so long.

It suddenly occurred to us that this was the way to think about what had happened to Jeff.

It all fit. We didn't find it hard to think of his death as a rescue—a deliverance out of bondage into freedom. That's what death becomes for everyone who calls on Jesus in faith. To all appearances death looks like an exit from the stage of life; from what we can see, it's just the final defeat in the battle to live, and in Jeff's case, it seemed like a thief that came early and stole the few years he might have had.

But Jesus' death and resurrection changed that scenario. Death is something different for those with faith in Jesus. He's changed it into an exodus out of this world and into the fullness of life. We wholeheartedly believed this and could see what a great deliverance it was for Jeff.

We could also believe that a huge tragic mistake could in reality have been a rescue operation organized by Jesus. God doesn't just come in after the fact and clean up the mess. The Bible represents Him as being in absolute control, sovereign over all things, shaping, restraining, allowing events to unfold in a way that always accomplishes His purpose. We could see how Jesus could have allowed this, even planned it for good.

And we could certainly understand where the enemy fit into the picture and how Jeff's overdose could be seen as a deliverance by God out of the hands of a deceiving oppressor. It made beautiful sense that Jesus would turn his death into a passage out of bondage into freedom—like the Israelites passing through the Red Sea, leaving the enemy frustrated and enraged on the other side.

But was he a prince? We could barely comprehend that this might actually be his true identity. Did God see him as a royal son in spite of his faint faith and his deep delusions? How could we know?

The question hinged on the nature of faith. Faith is looking away from ourselves and looking to Jesus. Faith connects us to Jesus and to all His benefits. All things come to us through Him. He is the source of our complete redemption, our identity as sons. Faith is all it takes. But could it be that those cries for help were faith enough?

The answer was "yes." It had to be. Otherwise we're all in trouble. That's what came to us as we considered the question. We cry for help to Jesus. Jesus does the rest. And if we could peek behind the curtain, we'd even see that He's the one who ensures the spell is not complete and then calls forth the cry for help.

Jeff's faith was weak. He didn't grasp reality for very long. His lucid moments of faith gave way to great confusion. But a weak faith is faith enough. Jesus may admonish us for being those of little faith, but He still rescues us with great love and power, and if that isn't true, none of us have any hope.

Jesus came into the world to save sinners. And we are sinners. When Rilian was under the spell of the witch, he was a decidedly unlovable character, utterly lacking in nobility or concern for anyone but himself. The character Jill was disgusted with him: "He's the silliest, most conceited selfish pig I've met for a long time."

The description works for Jeff but it also works for the rest of us. And yet Jesus considers us sons designated for rescue. All His anger is reserved for our Enemy, the Deceiver, the

Destroyer, the one who took us captive. He sets aside our sins as forgiven by virtue of His death and deals with us according to His love.

The marvel here is that not only do His ears pick up that little weak cry we utter in our sane moments, but He also then moves heaven and earth to answer it. To hear Jesus tell it, we are of such great value to Him that He drops everything and pours all His energies—even His life—into the rescue, and He doesn't give up until we're saved.

In *The Silver Chair*, when Aslan tells Jill the story of the prince, he starts with this fact: A king had a son who was stolen from him. Aslan gives Jill her assignment like it's the will of God: This prince must and shall be freed and restored to his father.

You pick up that same flavor of will and determination from the parables Jesus tells of lost things and how they *will be found* because they are God's own possessions. The young man may look like a punk kid, but in reality he's the son of the Father, a son who was stolen through the enchanting allure of the enemy, and *he will be saved.*

True for Jeff. True for us. It didn't escape our notice how like Jeff we were. How like the prince. We fall into forgetfulness like falling off a log. We're easily seduced by anything that strokes our vanity. None of us has the integrity of complete consistency. Who are we after all? What is our true identity? Thank God the Lord has the prerogative to answer the question. His death has put to death all but one of our identities.

He declares the person who cries for help to be the blessed and infinitely valuable child of God. Amongst our many multiple personalities, He says: "That's the real person, he's in his right mind when he's believing in Me, and that faith, however weak, will bring him home. I will see to it."

In the end everything else will fall away and we will be fully ourselves. We will wake as from a dream and enter into a glorious new reality because God has designated that we are sons and daughters who must and shall be saved, children whose ultimate transformation into our true identity is guaranteed.

But why didn't Jeff experience more of that transformation in this life? Why did he always seem to be stuck on the threshold, still wearing the remnants of his slavery? Why didn't he live more like a son?

Maybe it's that his faith never gained strength. Maybe it was never more than a cry uttered from the depths, in brief moments of desperate sanity, only to be swamped again by a towering wave of fear. His vision of Christ never grew into a transforming courage. Faith enables us to walk on water, but sometimes faith quails and we start to sink. Even then, Jesus reaches out and saves us just the same.

Then again, maybe Jeff is not the only one. None of us are fully transformed in this life; we're all groaning as we look for the great change to come upon us. We're all shaking off the spell, crying out for help, believing in and experiencing our redemption, but still waiting for the final full redemption.

Whatever the answer, we were reassured again and delivered into the sunlit lands. The old Jeff was gone and an awesome transformation into his true new self had come upon him. Anyone who is saved is saved completely because it's not about us—it's all about Jesus.

Finding Courage ...
in their words:

My dear friend Charles,

My heart was stabbed with pangs of compassion as I read the news of your Jeff's untimely death. I am so sorry for you and Janet, and wish that there was some way I could be of tangible support. You and your family will certainly be in my fervent prayers.

I thank the Lord that His wisdom, mercy and love see far beyond our mood swings and the fickle nature of our heart commitments to the reality of the new life He has sovereignly planted within us, and the beginnings of the transformation from old to new that He has promised to complete despite our tenacious fallen natures.

As Paul says so comfortingly, it was while we were still helpless and dead in our sins that Christ died for us.

Looking forward to hearing from you in due time, and lifting your heavy hearts to the throne of mercy.

I am your friend and brother in Christ,
Mateen

❧

Dear Mr. Morris,

I dont know if you would remember me or not but my name is D. and I sent in an e-mail last year when I lost my 8 year old son and mother within 2 months time along with losing my home 3 months after their loss. Both you and your director sent me correspondence.

I would like to take this time to tell you a bit more about myself. You see, I was and am a recovering drug addict. Drug addiction runs rampant in my family. At age 30 while my husband was in prison (he was a heroin addict) I became addicted to drugs.

I started doing drugs while I unknowingly had just conceived. Because of my drug use during the 1st trimester of my pregnancy my son was born with a heart condition. He was expected to live for 2 years; he lived to be 8 years old.

The story you told from "The Silver Chair" so reminded me of the dark days of drug addiction and how I too, during times of being a slave to that dark world, cried out to God to save me. I couldnt free myself either, the Lord had to help me.

You know, your letter made me realize how much I can still vacillate so widely. Maybe not in drugs but in other sins that I am still ensnared and you have given me much hope as to the Savior who will come and take us away.

I have spoken to a school for problem teens a few times, along with churches and at a women's prison to let them know the consequences of drug abuse and the effects it has on others. I know, as you do, that God can and does take the ugliest and most painful situations in our lives and make them into something beautiful. And OH I so pray that your son's departure to Glory will touch many hearts as it has mine and to make so many remember that God is greater than anything the Deceiver can try to take from us.

Thank you for your courage, strength and witness. You have touched me in a powerful way.

Every Blessing

D.

Charles Morris,

I just heard your commentary on the radio and was deeply touched and saddened at the death of your son. I know I cannot begin to understand or relate to that kind of pain and loss.

Your closing comments about the "rescue" meant a great deal to me. We have a rebellious teenage daughter.

Most of the time she lives behind a hardened exterior, rejecting her parents and God. There are times I want to get away from her—we both do. Every once in a while, however, there is a little window and we see a young girl crying out for love and understanding.

Our family has loved the Chronicles of Narnia for many years. I have never thought about "The Silver Chair" in quite the way you described. Thank you for this encouragement to persevere and keep on loving.

Susan

Finding Courage ...
in the Word:

PSALM 18:3–6, 16–17

I call to the LORD, who is worthy of praise, and I am saved from my enemies.

The cords of death entangled me; the torrents of destruction over-whelmed me.

The cords of the grave coiled around me; the snares of death confronted me.

In my distress I called to the LORD; I cried to my God for help. From his temple he heard my voice; my cry came before him, into his ears.

He reached down from on high and took hold of me; he drew me out of deep waters.

He rescued me from my powerful enemy, from my foes, who were too strong for me.

LUKE 15:20–24

So he got up and went to his father.

But while he was still a long way off, his father saw him and was filled with compassion for him; he ran to his son, threw his arms around him and kissed him.

The son said to him, "Father, I have sinned against heaven and against you. I am no longer worthy to be called your son."

But the father said to his servants, "Quick! Bring the best robe and put it on him. Put a ring on his finger and sandals on his feet.

"Bring the fattened calf and kill it. Let's have a feast and celebrate.

"For this son of mine was dead and is alive again; he was lost and is found."

So they began to celebrate.

2 CORINTHIANS 5:16–17

So from now on we regard no one from a worldly point of view. Though we once regarded Christ in this way, we do so no longer. Therefore, if anyone is in Christ, he is a new creation; the old has gone, the new has come!

1 JOHN 3:2

Dear friends, now we are children of God, and what we will be has not yet been made known. But we know that when he appears, we shall be like him, for we shall see him as he is.

4

Finding
Courage ...

in the
fellowship

FIVE DAYS A WEEK CHARLES GOES on the radio and says something about Jesus. When 9/11 hit, he made the decision to scrap all the prerecorded programs and go live, or close to it, and address the raw loss we all felt. He spoke directly to that here-and-now shock and testified that the gospel could stand up to it. Man-made towers collapse, but the Lord is a strong tower that never will.

From that day on, the program changed. Charles no longer recorded weeks in advance; he spoke fresh into the context of life as we live it, either together on the big scale or individually on the small scale.

The program for the Monday after Jeff's death had been recorded on Friday—a message about suicide Internet sites from

Japan where young people log on for expertise and advice on how to kill themselves. There's a growing demand.

Charles talked about Psalm 118, which describes the suicidal feeling of being surrounded with no way out. It goes on to tell how God is real and how he will meet you and deliver you into a "large place" (Psalm 118:5 NASB). He wanted to beam that possibility into the minds of kids who were thinking of killing themselves, to give them defiant words of faith so they could say to the Destroyer, "I will not die but live and tell of the works of the Lord." Of course, we'd been thinking about Jeff. We wanted to beam that hope directly into *his* heart and on Monday, when it aired, the mocking irony of it hit us.

On Tuesday's program Charles told the news of Jeff's death. "Our son did not live but died." It was our own personal 9/11 and it seemed to present a challenge, a kind of test, not of us, but of the things we'd been saying about Jesus. The questions it raised seemed to be hanging in the air, which meant we had an opportunity to testify: "Yes, the things we believe hold up; they don't collapse under these circumstances; they bear the weight of this; Jesus is real and enough. The gospel speaks to this—to the heart of it—like nothing else." Above all, it gave us an opportunity to testify to the ultimate message, "Christ supercedes everything. Even though, to all appearances, it may seem the Destroyer has succeeded and our hopes have been dashed, Jesus still triumphs. In spite of appearances, in spite of sin and weakness, because of Christ we believe that our son, though he died, yet lives."

After those programs people began to send us letters and e-mails full of love and comfort, many of them containing similar testimonies of the solid reality of the very present Lord. Our story is not unique of course; it's the common experience of believers finding the joy of Jesus more real than the pain of their circumstances.

On Wednesday, Peter, Suzanne, Charles, and I boarded a plane for Oklahoma. Kate, Rich, and the grandgirls were driving from Washington and we were all converging in Seminole.

Oklahoma in August is something else. When wind comes sweeping down the plains, it's like the air conditioner ran out of coolant and nothing but hot air blows at you. The cicadas whir all day long and the rustle of the scrub oaks actually sounds dusty as the languid afternoons go on and on. But now and then a cool wind comes sweeping in ahead of a thunderstorm and the smell of the coming rain suddenly becomes the real thing, pelting down in glorious relief. In climate-controlled places like Orange County, California, where we live now, you never get such grand reliefs—although we've yet to convince any Californians of this disadvantage.

A friend who came for the funeral from Colorado drew me aside later and asked me, tentatively, not wanting to be insulting but still wondering: "Why Seminole?"

Seminole is where Charles grew up. It's where all our children were born. If you want to go back even further, it's where the gushers erupted and an oil boom took off then died down and would have left behind a little ghost town if it hadn't been for enterprising citizens who've managed to keep things going. The oil industry brought Charles' father there to work, along with the hope that a change of climate would help his mother's severe asthma, which it didn't. She died when he was eight.

There's a family plot in the Maple Grove cemetery where I watched Jeff's birth father laid to rest after his car was struck by a truck one foggy morning when Jeff was eighteen months old and Kate was four.

Soon after, our bachelor friend Charles left his job with United Press International in Florida and moved back to manage the local FM station. He and I grew close in Seminole—the two of us making up the full complement of single adults in our little church. Seminole is where we eventually married, and Charles adopted Kate and Jeff and, four years later, Peter arrived, weighing in at 11 pounds 14 ounces and becoming a legend in the local doctor's lore.

As we stepped out of the revolving doors at the Will Rogers airport in Oklahoma City, and the windblown prairie heat suddenly sapped the air out of our lungs, we knew we were home. I remember coming out of the hospital in August to bring a newborn Jeffy home and being knocked back a step by that same wall of breathtaking heat. But this time something even more draining than the heat hit us—something that began to sap the energy of our faith.

First was Jeff's grandfather, who met us with a mask of grief on his face that seemed unanswerable. What could we say to him? His grandson was coming home in a box.

As we drove into that familiar little town, past the places that never seem to change, our hope just started to shrivel up. Death had conquered. A hometown life full of promise had been cut short, and we could do nothing to change it. Everywhere we went, we ran into old acquaintances who offered us well-meant but superficial condolences. "So sorry, so sad. I had a nephew, a cousin, a friend of my son's, who went the same way. Drugs."

The funeral-home visit was first priority because we had to quickly discuss and decide things. If you live in a small town, the funeral home becomes familiar territory. We'd been there count-less times for other deaths but this time it was our turn. Our turn to sit in the office and discuss clothes and when the body would arrive at the airport and how difficult it would be to make him look presentable after such a long time. Our turn to receive the special hushed treatment and choose a casket and look at those dreadful cushioned, satin interiors in either ivory or powder blue. All routine funeral-home business, but it's a nightmare when it's your son.

"Please God, don't let it be true, let us wake up."

But it was true and soon his body would be laid in the ground, and life would have to go on. It's not the funeral home's fault. Someone has to do the job. But as kind and sensitive as they may be, it's still a business and the down-pat process somehow diminishes both the monstrosity of death and the glory of the resurrection. Both end up painted in pastel colors with easy-listening music playing in the background. By the time the process ended, we were tranquilized, and miserable.

Later that day we took the drive around town. We always take the drive when we get back to Seminole—down Milt Phillips, turn on Reid Street, past the new First Baptist Church, then through the cemetery to relive a little history. After that we cruise Main, seeing which businesses have finally succumbed to Wal-Mart, and then head back to Milt Philips, sometimes stopping to get a cherry limeade at Sonic.

This time memories of Jeff's childhood came flooding in as we drove. We passed Taco Casa where he always ordered a cheese sancho with extra cheese, and the snow cone stand where he and Kate and Pete would stand sweltering in line until a young attendant thrust the paper cones full of ice and flavored syrup through the little window and into their hands.

We went past the house where at age two Jeff followed our cocker spaniel over the chain-link fence and was spotted by a neighbor playing in her backyard sandbox, oblivious to his bleeding palms. We could see him as a little Bo or Luke out in the garage in his Cozy Coupe imagining he was one of the Dukes of Hazzard. We remembered how after our wedding, he gallantly offered to sleep with Mommy and let Charles have his nice twin bed. The birthdays and Sunday-school papers and fireworks in his grandparent's backyard with cold Chocolate Soldiers to drink and hamburgers on the grill—all those happy times now seemed shrouded with unbearable sadness.

Reliving the past felt like watching a Greek drama unfold, knowing the characters are heading inexorably toward a tragic end. You want to shout out to them and warn them to change their course but they can't hear you. You feel sorry for them because they're so cheerfully oblivious to their future. The poor things don't know that their little, beloved son will end up dead on a bathroom floor, wasted and broken and beyond the reach of their protection. The reality seemed remote; we were numb, but excruciating stabs of pain kept fighting through and killing us.

Where was our joy? Where was our comfort? We were drying up like prairie grass in August. We tried to reconstruct it in our hearts, but we knew it was only self-talk, not Spirit-given conviction. We cried out to Jesus, not just for help but for Jesus Himself, and in His great kindness, He answered. But then the waves would break over us again as we viewed Jeff's body, read the cards on the flowers, thanked the ladies who brought the food, talked about headstones and death certificates, greeted heartsick family members.

Each encounter, each hug, each meeting of the eyes, meant we had to say something, we had to offer some take on this thing, and we wanted it to be a testimony to Jesus. But the words that came out of our mouths sounded hollow and unconvincing. Our minds and hearts were being co-opted against our will into a realm where everything we believed seemed diminished and unreal.

We were in *The Silver Chair* all over again, and we clearly needed outside reinforcements. They came—or rather, were sent—in the form of beautiful believing friends. First came Cyndi and Lanning, drawn as they told us later by a love for us that was so motivating they didn't even question it. They heard where the funeral was going to be, and they got in their car and drove and drove and drove across great empty stretches from their home in Colorado Springs to where we were in Seminole.

We arranged to meet in Braum's—a fluorescent-lit ice-cream place with big booths where we figured we'd be able to talk with some degree of privacy. We drove there with a kind of desperation we couldn't put into words. We craved more than just friendly faces—we'd seen many kind and friendly faces, faces of people who loved us. It wasn't just Cyndi and Lanning, as dear as they were. We needed something else, and when we saw them, we realized what it was—their faith. We needed their faith.

What a sight they were to our hungry eyes—Jesus was written all over them. A surge of strength came to us just from hugging them in the parking lot. We didn't have to tell them what Jesus had done for Jeff—they knew. It was like talking to someone who's seen the same magnificent sight you've seen—when words fail and you can't describe it, it's okay because they know. They've seen it too. They can finish your sentences for you.

We got our cups of coffee and slid into a booth. Lanning had been Jeff's Sunday-school teacher, and as I sat there tearing my napkin into tiny little pieces, he laughed and said it was just like

Jeff. He'd dealt with Jeff's fidgets, he appreciated his quirky wit, and he'd also been the recipient of some of his paranoid phone calls when he was literally out of his mind. He'd invested hours of heartbreaking, frustrating attempts to help him.

Lanning knew Jeff pretty well inside out, and he loved him just the same and confirmed for us that Jeff's faith in Jesus was real. He even told us about times when Jeff's faith had strengthened his own. Of course, we knew it was only Lanning's humility and kindness allowing him to have a take like that on Jeff, but we also knew Jesus gave him that take. The Spirit had given him eyes to see Jeff, not as he was "in the flesh" as the Bible says, but as the new creation he was in Jesus. Needless to say, his words were a salve to our wounded hearts.

But they didn't just bring us faith in Jeff's salvation and his ultimate well-being—they brought something bigger—something that contained comfort about Jeff like the universe contains stars. They brought with them, all the way from Colorado, their apprehension of Jesus, the crucified Jesus, as the central fact of existence. His death made atonement for us; His resurrection made a new creation for us. Cyndi and Lanning's faith opened our eyes to see it again, to live in it again, and from there, everything looks different.

We'd been experiencing the other world, where Jesus is considered irrelevant to most of life, and everything operates according to what can be seen. It's a hopeless, deluded place, but their faith woke us up so we could drink in the morning again.

We felt like the prodigal son waking up from a bad dream and realizing we're not fending for ourselves in the pigsty anymore; we're home safe in our Father's house where love reigns, the past is forgotten and everything has been provided.

A small divine "coincidence" emerged during that conversation with Lanning and Cyndi. We were trying to explain why it was so wonderful for them to be there. We said it was like Paul writing to the believers in Rome telling them he couldn't wait to see them and be mutually strengthened by each other's faith. The last few days had made us realize this wasn't just Paul's nice way of saying, "It would be great to see you." He was talking about a spiritual reality—an empowerment to believe. Cyndi's jaw dropped and she leaned forward and said, "We talked about that same verse all the way here. It was our theme verse—the reason we came. We didn't know what we could do for you, but we thought maybe just being with you would encourage your faith. We felt like we were on a mission, not just to make you feel loved, but to actually help put courage into you."

The refreshing rains of believing friends fell on our dry hearts. And the showers continued to sweep in, one downpour after another, relieving the drought, bringing comfort. Our friends Jeff and Sue climbed into their car and drove the same long road as Lanning and Cyndi across the plains from Colorado to Oklahoma. We rendezvoused with them the next night, again at Braum's, and talked about Jesus. Richard's parents came from

Oregon and brought Dick's pastoral kindness and Christie's energetic love into the situation. And on the day of the funeral, a contingent of men Charles had known for years came from Oklahoma City, brothers in Christ. They walked into the chapel like reinforcements arriving on the day of battle and took their seats on the front row, a solid force of faith and love.

Courage, it turns out, comes from being together with believers.

Finding Courage ...
in their words:

Dear Charles and Janet,

I am a listener to Haven and I want you to know that you will be in my prayers these days and weeks ahead. While I have not had to walk this most-difficult road, I know many who have.

Especially one lady—both her children are in heaven. She is coming up on the one-year anniversary of her son's death after her daughter's death a year before. There is no way we can begin to carry her pain—but her heart's cry is **"The Lord is enough!"** She just said the other day, that if the Lord were not enough, she would not be able to go on. Her life is full of terrible heartache and pain ... and yet she is the most radiant Christian in our large church. She stands strong and tall and firm that there are no mistakes with Him, and that...

"The Lord is enough."

May you find the all-sufficiency of Christ, through the power of the Holy Spirit, to the glory of God—to be what carries you through this incredible pain.

In His Love,

Joyce

Dearest Charles and Janet,

Julie just called and forwarded news of Jeff's passing. Words simply pale in comparison to the feelings coursing through our hearts right now. We both so desire to just reach out and comfort you both ... to wrap our arms around you and hold on.

As I write this, Cyndi and I are seeking gentle harmony in prayer and conversation—mostly sharing precious memories of Jeff and how he touched our lives. I am so very thankful that God used Jeff so powerfully, especially when he would remind me to pray with him during our numerous late-night telephone conversations. He never failed to ask the most incredible questions either! And In the midst of enduring tremendous personal struggle, he would always think to ask of ways in which to encourage or pray for _me_. I always felt humbled by that ... it was as if the Lord was lovingly reminding me that my need for mercy was equal to his. So much for my being Jeff's teacher—in many ways, I learned from him.

Before I go, I'd like to ask if you could pass on details regarding the services to be held in

Oklahoma. Location and time is all that we require, as we are attempting to work out arrangements to attend if possible. Lastly, Cyndi has a few words to share....

[Cyndi] My heart is breaking for you and the sorrow you must feel now. Janet, I remember the long conversation that we had just a few weeks ago about Jeff and your faith that God was faithful in saving your son. And I am confident that He has, even in Jeff's death, delivered him unto Himself—whole and healed in spirit, mind and body. I believe Jeff was in a civil war— two opposing forces residing in the same "country" that warred against the other in an effort to dominate. The struggle is over, Jeff is home, and God is sovereign and victorious. I will always remember the precious things about Jeff that we will miss—his humor and his kindness toward us. We have always been touched by the unconditional and sacrificial love that you two continually demonstrated toward Jeff, and we know that Jeff saw it, too. You gave out of the love that Christ poured into your hearts, and by that love, Jeff knew of the Savior's love for him as well.

We love you both and we ask that you convey our love and sympathy to Peter and Katie also—
God's comfort and peace be with you,
Lanning and Cyndi

Dear Charles and Janet,

We arrived home from some days away to find your email. At a time like this an email seems impersonal but it is the quickest way of letting you know from England that we are sharing in your grief and are praying for you.

Words are so inadequate when what we really want to do is put our arms around you and hug you. We pray that you will know the loving arms of Jesus around you both and the whole family.

We wept as we read your email and I still do as I write this reply. Yet our hearts have that same assurance; that Jeff is with the Lord and that in His mercy all is well.

As I prayed for the words to say to you I have been reminded of one of Matt's songs.

The words are:

I have heard so many songs / Listened to a thousand tongues / But there is one that sounds above them all / The Father's song, the Father's love / You sung it over me / And for all eternity it's written on my heart. Heaven's perfect melody / The Creator's symphony / You are singing over me The Father's song. Heaven's perfect mystery / The King of love has sent for me / And now You're singing over me / The Father's song.

We are sure that the Father is singing his song of love and compassion over all of you. We continue to pray that you will know the comfort and sustaining power of God's loving presence now and in the coming days.

We do love you and are praying for you.

With our love in Jesus

David & Jenny

Finding Courage ...
in the Word:

MALACHI 3:16

Then those who feared the LORD talked with each other, and the LORD listened and heard. A scroll of remembrance was written in his presence concerning those who feared the LORD and honored his name.

ROMANS 1:11–12

I long to see you so that I may impart to you some spiritual gift to make you strong—that is, that you and I may be mutually encouraged by each other's faith.

COLOSSIANS 1:3–5

We always thank God, the Father of our Lord Jesus Christ, when we pray for you, because we have heard of your faith in Christ Jesus and of the love you have for all the saints—the faith and love that spring from the hope that is stored up for you in heaven.

1 THESSALONIANS 3:7–9

Therefore, brothers, in all our distress and persecution we were encouraged about you because of your faith. For now we really live, since you are standing firm in the Lord. How can we thank God enough for you in return for all the joy we have in the presence of our God because of you?

1 THESSALONIANS 5:10–11

He died for us so that, whether we are awake or asleep, we may live together with him. Therefore encourage one another and build each other up, just as in fact you are doing.

HEBREWS 10:25

*Let us not give up meeting together, as some are in the habit of
doing, but let us encourage one another—and all the more as you
see the Day approaching.*

5

Finding Courage ...

in death's presence

I WOKE UP SLOWLY, EMERGING UNDEFENDED out of a dreamless sleep, and then I remembered: Jeff is dead. Today is his funeral.

We were sleeping on the sofa bed in my in-laws' front living room. The room was dark but even so, the inexorable sunlight of that day was working its way through the crack in the drapes. I lay there and thought, "Well, I can't do it."

The prospect of walking through the long day ahead daunted me. I went one by one through the things we'd planned: meeting at Poppie's house with Kate and family, loading into the funeral cars, going through the service at the cemetery chapel, walking to the grave for those final words then home for eating and greeting. An overwhelming prospect, but it was my part in the funeral I knew I couldn't face and yet I couldn't face shrinking from it either.

We had decided to do the funeral ourselves. It made sense that if we were the ones who could speak firsthand of Jeff's precious value and if we were the ones who'd felt the Lord's profound comfort, then we should do the talking. I guess we just instinctively wanted to erect a memorial of spoken words that would testify to Jeff's redemption. And we wanted to minister the comfort we'd been given, to reassure the people who were mourning for us. We also didn't want to sink under anyone else's diminished message that would weaken our courage.

We'd made plans for our son-in-law, Richard, to lead the service and speak at the graveside, and for Charles, Kate, and me each to have a part in the service. And that was the impossibility I woke up to that morning. I don't know how the others felt, but to me it didn't seem doable.

I wasn't worried about breaking down into tears. I was worried because every time I get into a situation where I'm supposed to speak in front of people, I'm like a deer frozen in the headlights. I'm fearless beforehand when I'm planning what to say. But the minute I get up there, all existence narrows down to one single point—me—standing all alone. The spotlight singles me out, and every eye watches me in suspended judgment. The crowd waits expectantly and every brilliant thing I planned to say mutates into something stupid. All the nice visions of being edifying or entertaining completely vanish, and I plow through my words like a person under torture; my one remaining goal is to get it over with. Then I sit down and for a long time I'm not aware of anything except my pounding heart. This is not an exaggeration.

My instinctive default mode in situations where something impossible but inevitable looms ahead is to rally my resources the best I can. Lying there that morning it came to me that gutting it out—or bailing out—were not my only options. Jesus offered Himself to me as a refuge, and I stepped into Him like someone stepping out of a screaming storm into a solid, well-built shelter. "How blessed are those who take refuge in Him." Instantly every-thing was still, the noise and danger stayed on the outside, and I was inside, sheltered and protected. The storm I stepped out of was my fear and isolation, and the refuge was Jesus Himself. "You hide me in the secret place of Your presence." I was tucked away safe and sound, and Jesus simply took care of everything.

The day began with a strange little event. Before we left for Poppie's house, I was searching around for a scrap of paper where I'd jotted down something I wanted to say. I thought I saw it way down under the very back of the sofa bed and, reaching my hand through, barely got hold of it with my fingers and pulled it out. It wasn't my note.

It was a handmade bookmark—in Jeff's handwriting—and he must have made it when he was thirteen, the last time he'd slept there. "Bookmark" was written at the top and underneath "The Lord of the Rings." When he was in junior high, he'd read

Tolkien's trilogy straight through and then straight through again. The bookmark was decorated with elfin runes, and one corner had Jeff's signature chew marks. But what grabbed me was the quote he'd written.

> "Where shall I find courage?"
> Frodo asked, "For that is what
> I chiefly need."

Frodo asked that question of an elf just as he was beginning his quest, full of trepidation, aware of the dark powers pursuing him, and acutely aware of his own littleness and inadequacy.

Three thoughts came to me as I held that little piece of paper.

One was how very odd it was that I had found this bookmark ten years later on the day of Jeff's funeral. The timing seemed heavy with significance. Recently a Florida hurricane took an unexpected turn, and on the news a man whose house had been spared at the last minute was interviewed: "If I didn't know better," he said, "I'd say it was providence." Well, I didn't know better and this seemed like providence to me.

The second thought was wrenching—to think of Jeff embarking on adolescence with that fear-filled reluctance—to think of him full of anxiety and wondering where to find courage. I could barely stand it. Who knows if he was experiencing all of that when he made the bookmark? In retrospect it seemed to sum up the major theme running through his life—he was fear-racked and in need of courage.

The third was that this was the exact question we kept posing to ourselves since Jeff's death, "Where can we find courage?" That was our chief need. We knew acutely how little and weak we were, how overcome by grief, how prone to darkness. We knew the answer to this question, but it was so easy to forget. We had to learn it again and again, and it always came down to Jesus. He'd been giving us bracing doses of courage all along the way, opening our eyes to see the things He'd accomplished, giving us profound reassurances. The bedrock of courage is Jesus—His death and resurrection, His love, His intentions toward us, the resources we have in Him, the future He has secured for us, but we have to see these things. They have to blaze into our darkness by the power of the Holy Spirit—which He gives us in answer to prayer.

He gave us courage through the fellowship of friends—the same way Frodo received courage from his friends. Like the fellowship of the ring, we had true-blue comrades who wouldn't let us go down the road alone.

In the gray hours of that morning, I had been asking the question again, "How will I find courage to live through this day?" I found it by taking refuge in Jesus, in knowing that I didn't have to function in isolation, drawing on my own depleted reserves, dealing with impossible situations like an orphan with no one to help. I was in Christ and His Spirit was in me.

Later, when the funeral cars pulled up in front of the little stone chapel in the middle of the cemetery and we disembarked, I was very conscious of being in that refuge. True, walking into the building momentarily startled me, seeing that the room was crammed full of people, and then being ushered to our places on the front row with every face looking on with hushed sympathy. That was my cue to freeze up in self-conscious fear, to see that crowd of friends and family as an audience I wanted to please, a panel of judges who would score my performance, or a skeptical jury that would take my testimony into consideration and make a judgment. But it didn't happen. I tell you this as one reporting a miracle.

The secret presence of Jesus is a refuge from preoccupation with the opinions of other people. I was in that fear-free zone, loved by Jesus, counting on His help, and only caring about what He thought about me, which meant I had an entirely different response when I saw those faces. My heart went out to them because their hearts were going out to us. I wanted to thank them for loving Jeff and tell them how deeply Jesus had comforted us.

We sat down on the front row and three feet in front of us, flanked by flowers, was Jeff's casket, with the podium elevated on a platform behind it. Richard opened the service, then Charles got up to speak, then me, then Kate.

We all basically said the same thing, which boiled down to Jeff—completely loved, completely lost, completely saved by Jesus. We all spoke of sorrow and joy, with joy holding the trump card. Even though the others don't suffer from stage fright, we all could have been overwhelmed with heartbreak and defeat. We all could have felt our words to be just empty talk, especially with the visible evidence of death right in front of us, the lid shut and sealed and draped with a saddle of yellow roses. Each of us had to stand behind Jeff's casket and talk over it, talk past it. And that's what happened, not just in the obvious physical sense, but in a spiritual sense as well. Faith came on strong by the power of the Holy Spirit. His presence was with us and He gave us the courage to face down Jeff's death, to believe in His redemption, and to speak it out loud and clear.

When Charles went up, he greeted practically everyone there as if each one were the guest of honor. There was nothing fake in this—my love for people may barely eke out, but his is brimful of kindness and goodwill. People are his great interest, and he enjoys them individually with a genuine, overflowing enthusiasm. Looking out on that group, Charles was unselfconsciously surveying a room full of priceless treasure.

He also honored Jeff's natural dad, who had been his closest friend and said what a privilege it had been to be Jeff's father for twenty years—a privilege, but an ongoing sorrow that left us helpless and crying out to the Lord. The natural thing would be to see his death as the final heartbreaking kibosh on all our hopes. "Not so," he said. "The Lord has been giving us great comfort that, *by his grace alone,* Jeff's death can be seen as something very different than that." He told the story of *The Silver Chair* and explained how we had come to believe that the Mighty One had organized a rescue for our son.

Then it was my turn.

We'd been in London years back and managed to get last-minute tickets to see *Les Miserables*. I remember a scene where the unwed mother, Fantine, is sick and dying from the degraded attempts she'd made to save her child from poverty and death. Desperately hanging on to life until Jean Valjean, the hero, arrives, she entreats him to redeem her beloved Cosette. Only when he gives his solemn promise to intercede and take her child as his own daughter is she able to pass on in peace. I cried hysterically, identifying with Fantine in that scene. Now as I looked out, I saw many dear people who'd made a stab at being a redeemer for Jeff—they had loved him and valued him—but none of us had been able to save him. Only Jesus has the power and the resources to completely and efficaciously redeem. I thanked them but I mainly wanted to thank Jesus for being that strong Redeemer of my son and that's what I did—without an ounce of nervousness because I was safe inside the Refuge.

Kate spoke last. "I miss Jeff," she said, "I miss my brother.

"I miss his love and his sense of humor. He knew me in ways that no one else will ever know me. Of course, he had a little brother's gift for knowing how to infuriate his sister. But he also listened to my woes and even slept on the floor in my room when I didn't want to be alone. He was the best of friends.

"The other side of Jeff's life was his struggle. He struggled more than anyone I've ever known and probably more than any of us will ever understand. He struggled with his body and his mind. Some of these things he was born with and some he did to himself.

"But there's something even more important about Jeff—he repented of his sins and trusted in Christ's death for salvation. Many times he would pore over his Bible and cry out for God to rescue him, which means that everything Jeff needed, the answer to all his struggles, belonged to him in Jesus. Jesus paid the price. Jesus is everything. He's 'wisdom from God and righteousness and sanctification and redemption.'

"A few months ago, when I found out Jeff was using drugs again, I fell on my knees and begged God to be merciful: 'He's my brother, he's my brother, please, You have to save him from himself.'

"I know that when Jeff died, God answered my prayer. Jeff is home and free. I'll see him again and when I do, he'll be a new person because the struggle is over for him. He'll be my sweet little brother, only much, much closer and much, much sweeter. God's grace goes deep, deep, deeper than we can ever fathom."

After Kate finished and the last song was sung, we walked out to the grave and Richard read from First Corinthians 15, each word ringing out with hope:

> Listen, I tell you a mystery: We
> will not all sleep, but we will all
> be changed—

in a flash, in the twinkling of
an eye, at the last trumpet.
For the trumpet will sound, the
dead will be raised imperishable, and we will be changed.
For the perishable must clothe
itself with the imperishable, and
the mortal with immortality.
When the perishable has been
clothed with the imperishable,
and the mortal with immortality,
then the saying that is written
will come true: "Death has
been swallowed up in victory.
Where, O death, is your victory? Where, O death, is your
sting?"
The sting of death is sin, and
the power of sin is the law. But
thanks be to God! He gives us
the victory through our Lord
Jesus Christ.

If we were to chisel a memorial to the day of Jeff's funeral, it
would read, "Jesus took care of everything." The power of His
resurrection came through loud and clear.

Finding Courage ...
in their words:

Dear Janet, Charles & Peter,

We are praying for you—especially today. You dear ones, we grieve with you as you remember your precious son and brother.

I was thanking God that Jeff is completely healed, restored, and comforted. God also offers peace to those who are far and those who are near. What a promise. It seems like Jeff alternated between being far and near, just as we all do. But God is higher than we are. He intercedes. Is. 26:12 says that He will establish peace for us since He has also performed for us all our works. His ways are not our ways. They are infinitely superior and merciful. I'm praying that God's faithfulness and strength will comfort you as you mourn this greatest loss.

Love,

Linda

Dear Charles,

Deb and I prayed for you and Janet this morning. I am so sorry. I came across these lines from "The Contemporary Christian" by John Stott (page 124), that struck me as a wonderful comfort:

"On seven separate occasions in the Gospels Jesus was 'moved with compassion,' for example toward the hungry and leaderless crowds, the widow of Nain, leprosy sufferers and a blind beggar. And in John 11.35 we read that 'Jesus wept'—not tears of anger in the face of death but tears of sympathy for the bereaved sisters. Is it not beautiful to see Jesus, when confronted by death and bereavement, so deeply moved? He felt indignation in the face of death, and compassion towards its victims."

God is with you, is moved by your pain, and loves you as you mourn. May His comfort be so very real to you throughout the days ahead.

Your friend in Christ,
David

Shalom Charles and Janet,

We've been praying for you and your family. I write sobbing with tears in my eyes and share a small portion of your grief. I can barely write. A friend who heard the radio program told me the news. I know God moved my heart deeply to pray.

I'm so glad to have known Jeff. It was so good to talk with him and hang out when I visited last. I am convinced of his salvation, too, based on our conversation at that time. I thought you might want to know this. He clearly told me that he previously hadn't been a Christian and that he had come to faith. I'm confident he will be there with our Lord Jesus when we arrive.

Again, we will continue to pray. I don't get to see you often, but you have a very special place in my heart.

In Messiah's Love,
Fred

Dear Charles Morris,

While listening to the radio I heard that you lost your son this last weekend, probably due to drugs and alcohol. My deepest sympathies are with you and family. Exactly one year ago, I almost died a very similar fate but instead I came to know Jesus Christ as my Lord and Savior. I thought sharing my experience, my testimony, may be of some value at this time.

I almost died from alcoholism early last August. I came home from work, determined to get drunk and to go out on the town although for some strange reason I said a prayer right before I went out. I got totally blitzed and don't remember exactly how I got home, but what I do remember is that as I was driving up the steep dirt road to my house on the hill, I just got totally mad at everything and put my foot all the way down on the accelerator, not caring if I crashed off the side of the hill and died.

Next thing I knew it was the next morning. I woke up, basically wondering how I had survived the night before. For some reason I went out to my vehicle, and embedded in the front grate of my Ford Explorer were all these wood chips. They were really wedged in there ... it took some effort to get them out, which led me to believe that I had crashed someplace and that I should have been dead.

A realization came over me that someone, that one being Jesus Christ, had died for my sins. Those wood chips in the front of the Explorer represented His cross to me, that Jesus had intervened to die for my sins. And that the wood chips broken into pieces represented His resurrection, that Jesus had arisen from the dead, even though His body had been broken by the cross. I cannot tell you how or why this occurred to me. I had not been reading the Bible, nor did I attend church at the time; God works miracles.

If my experience and testimony may be of any use to you, or to others, feel free to use my story.

Yours in Christ,

Marcus

Finding Courage ...
in the Word:

2 SAMUEL 22:30

With your help I can advance against a troop; with my God I can scale a wall.

PSALM 5:11

Let all who take refuge in you be glad; let them ever sing for joy. Spread your protection over them, that those who love your name may rejoice in you.

PSALM 9:9–10

The LORD is a refuge for the oppressed, a stronghold in times of trouble. Those who know your name will trust in you, for you, LORD, have never forsaken those who seek you.

PSALM 27:5

For in the day of trouble he will keep me safe in his dwelling; he will hide me in the shelter of his tabernacle and set me high upon a rock.

PSALM 31:19

How great is your goodness, which you have stored up for those who fear you, which you bestow in the sight of men on those who take refuge in you.

PSALM 34:22

The LORD redeems his servants; no one will be condemned who takes refuge in him.

PSALM 57:1

I will take refuge in the shadow of your wings until the disaster has passed.

PSALM 59:16–17

> I will sing of your strength, in the morning I will sing of your love;
> for you are my fortress, my refuge in times of trouble.
> O my Strength, I sing praise to you; you, O God, are my fortress, my
> loving God.

ROMANS 15:13

> May the God of hope fill you with all joy and peace as you trust
> in him, so that you may overflow with hope by the power of the
> Holy Spirit.

6

Finding Courage ...

in a friend

WRAPPED IN AN AFGHAN AGAINST THE CHILL of Poppie's air-conditioned house, I was resting in the spare bedroom, savoring moments from Charlotte and Grace's little birthday celebration like chocolates from a box. The original idea had been for us to celebrate the grandgirls' August birthdays in Washington where they live. Jeff's death scuttled the plan but since their other grandparents, Dick and Christie, had come to Oklahoma for the funeral, we all went into gear and threw a little party anyway.

At three, Charlotte loved crocodiles with a great love. Kate thinks it started with *Peter Pan* and the crocodile creeping up on Captain Hook with that menacing alarm clock ticking away inside of him. The theory is that Charlotte dealt with the scariness of it by recreating crocodiles into something wonderful in her imagination. However it happened, her affection for croco-diles ran deep (not *alligators*, Nana!), so crocodiles it was. We draped a string of crocodile lights around the table for decoration (yes, it's possible to find crocodile lights if you are a grand-mother), and Christie's gift of a giant inflatable crocodile soon floated in Poppie's swimming pool. Katie set out the party plates and napkins and brought in a grocery-store sheetcake laden with gobs of food-color icing. One-year-old Gracie's burning passion ran to cake and ice cream, which she plowed into with both chubby hands while cameras flashed and a gallery of parents and grandparents and great-grandparents (and Uncle Peter) beamed our love. I was replaying it all in my mind, smiling over these delicious moments, when suddenly—I remembered Jeff—and went from blissful Nana to stricken mother in a single heartbeat.

These precious untrammeled lives juxtaposed with Jeff's trampled-down, destroyed life were just so … what? I don't think there's a word for it, no adjective that really captures a mother's anguish when she can't save her children, when she has to help-lessly stand by and watch them being led away into captivity. The prophet Jeremiah talks about Rachel weeping for her children and refusing to be comforted because they are no more. I think the "refusing to be comforted" gets at the heart of it. If her child is wounded, a mother bleeds, and she doesn't stop bleeding until the Lord staunches the wound.

Suddenly I was a wounded and bleeding mother who desper-ately needed the Lord. Again. Even at the best of times my need for His grace is new every morning, and lo and behold, there it is again, every afternoon. This was certainly not the best of times. Thankfully He never tires of pouring it on.

My friend Linda and I were sitting on the beach one sun-drenched day a few months ago, watching the waves roll in, one after the other. She suddenly exclaimed, "Lord, those waves are just like your mercies; they never stop coming!" I followed up with a heartfelt, "Amen!" Seeing the Lord's grace applied to new situations makes it perpetually fresh and glorious, like new waves washing in. My grief was perpetually a "new situation"—it just kept happening all over again. And His grace just kept coming, every time, without fail.

My lament that evening went something like this: "How can I bear it Lord? My poor thrown-away child, absent from the family party, friendless and forgotten, even by his mother the very day after his funeral." Even though Jeff was gone, I still had the same feeling I'd had his whole life—as if only my love stood between him and utter oblivion—as if I had to keep him safe by loving him intentionally and unwaveringly, never giving up, always holding him in the front of my mind. If your mother forgets you, then you're truly lost, really gone, right out of existence.

I'd read once about street children in Peru, living in pasteboard boxes, many of them sent away by their parents because they couldn't afford to feed them. They call them *desechables,* Spanish for "disposables" or "throwaways." Jeff had been so close to being a *desechable,* especially the time we asked him to leave home because of his incorrigible drug use and his refusal to go into rehab. So close, but not thrown away, not forgotten, not as long as he was a "son" and someone's heart remembered him and counted him as infinitely valuable—someone like his mother. I understand now why people want to erect memorials to the dead and etch their lost lives in stone, swearing, "We will never forget." I feared forgetting. My heart broke with the thought of forgetting Jeff.

In the quiet, after I'd cried my heart out, words came washing in, sweet, often-read words: "Can a mother forget the child at her breast? Even if she could forget, I will not forget you. See, you are engraved on the palms of my hands." They were words from Isaiah spoken by the Lord to His people when they thought He'd forgotten them. And they were words to me, lifting the impossible responsibility for keeping Jeff from being forgotten off of my shoulders. It wasn't my love; it was the Lord's love for Jeff that was able to keep him from being a *desechable,* a forgotten one. His never-forgetting love for His own was more unwavering, more unquenchable, than any finite mother's love.

My love was just a flimsy little tack, never really strong enough to keep Jeff from falling, but the Lord's love was etched with saving power on the palms of His hands. I thought about the nails that pounded into the flesh of Jesus, making indelible marks of love, and how that engraving will never be removed, and

I realized—the love of Jesus engulfs mine like the ocean swallows a raindrop. The mother-quality of it staggered me and gave me great relief from the strain of trying to keep Jeff safe with the strength of my own love—as if I could. Jesus is like a mother—a mother who would never dream of locking up when only two of her three children are in for the night. He has to have them all home safe and the party can't begin until everyone is present and accounted for. Each one is engraved on the palms of His hands by name, and the strength of His love is able to bring them home—a thing I could never do for Jeff.

This was deep consolation to me—but I wasn't through crying yet. So many painful memories suddenly opened up like wounds and bled freely, years of pain for Jeff. I needed to hear how the Lord would answer them. "He died so friendless, Lord, with no one returning his calls, no one sticking by him like a brother."

I don't know Jeff's story from the inside, but as his mother I watched from the outside, and I saw his deep, lifelong need for a true friend. Johnny was his first little buddy, when they were just three and four years old. I found an old picture of John at the age of four still tucked away amongst Jeff's few remaining possessions even though they hadn't seen or talked to each other for seventeen years. Then there was Tommy in kindergarten and first grade—a big guy always getting into trouble. Jeff's loyalty went so deep that he confessed to pouring milk into another boy's locker when Tommy was actually to blame. He was heartbroken to find out later that in a separate interview with the teacher, Tommy had blamed it on Jeff. In the end it was all straightened out, and Tommy admitted being the milk culprit, later apologizing to Jeff with a laugh and a "Hey, what was I gonna do?" Jeff understood.

He had other best friends but none of them seemed to hold the friendship as dear as Jeff. He would make excuses for his friends and credit them with a loyalty they never really had. It broke my heart, and it was breaking my heart even more now as I thought about the deep loneliness he must have felt just six days ago, the morning he died, when none of his friends had returned his calls the week before.

Sobbing and sobbing does finally ease the ache a little, and I felt ready to have Jesus wipe the tears away. Jesus came to comfort those who mourn and His comfort is very real and personal. Jesus ministered to each of the people crowding around Him, with tears streaming down their faces, holding out their afflictions, as if they were the only ones in the world who'd ever grieved. He was and is the Savior and that title encompasses all the grief this world has to offer. Surely He would know how to relieve a mother grieving for the friendlessness of her son.

Jesus, comfort one who mourns.

My Bible was in my lap, unopened because I'd gotten distracted ruminating over the birthday party and then ended up collapsed in pain for Jeff. Opening it now felt solemn, the words were alive, God's words, not merely recorded for posterity but spoken by Him into the present moment. I scanned the Psalms,

looking for the one about being hurt by faithless friends, and
found Psalm 41:9:

> Even my close friend, whom I
> trusted, he who shared my
> bread, has lifted up his heel
> against me.

With a jolt I recognized the verse as one Jesus applied to Himself
when Judas betrayed Him. Jesus experienced a profound betrayal by
His friends. He knew the great pain of being abandoned by friends
in a time of need, of dying friendless. It wasn't just Judas who
betrayed Him; He told the whole crowd "you will all desert me" and
they did and so have I, and so did Jeff, again and again.

I thought, "Why did He willingly enter into this grief? I
mean, He comes into the world, the glorious, holy Son of God,
and just starts being a friend to us. He shares his bread with us;
He talks to us heart to heart; He hangs around with us. He was
'a friend of tax collectors and sinners.'"

I remembered Jesus saying to the disciples, "Our friend
Lazarus has fallen asleep." I was awestruck to think that the Son
of God would say "our friend"—that He would create a circle of
friends and include us in it and then make Himself vulnerable to
rejection like any man who gives himself in friendship. And He
did it knowing full well it meant He'd end up being hurt and
betrayed by His friends.

Why? Why would He choose to be our friend? Why would He enter into our suffering, even the suffering of friendlessness, and experience it with us? We're left shaking our heads—or falling on our knees—because it's too deep to fathom. But this we can know—He *is* our friend—He said so Himself in John's Gospel: "You are no longer servants for I have called you friends." Jesus is our one true Friend who stands by us all the way to death when other friends say, "I'm outta here." Like a best Friend, He shares all his deepest confidences with us, not withholding anything. Deuteronomy 13:6 (NASB) talks about a "friend who is as your own soul." He chose not just to be *our* Friend, but to consider us *His* friends—friends who are as His own soul.

The issue then was not that Jesus didn't give Jeff a friend—He gave Himself as Jeff's Friend. The issue was that Jeff hadn't been a faithful friend to His best Friend, Jesus, as none of us have been. And yet, like the friend our hearts crave, He forgives us. More than that, when we are a faithless Tommy who sells him out to save our own skin and excuse ourselves with a "What was I gonna to do?"—He takes the blame for our faithlessness onto Himself and pays the price. He is a true Friend. He puts aside all our betrayals and keeps the friendship intact, without a rift. "Greater love has no one than this, that he lay down his life for his friends" (John 15:13). So said Jesus on the night before His death, as He looked at those men with His staggering love, those friends who would all desert Him as He was laying down His life for them.

The Bible has a way of getting the real question out on the table. We go with one question and the Bible counters with another question.

The question I had been asking was, "What do You have to say to me about my son dying so friendless?"

The question I ended up asking was, "How could Jesus be such a true Friend to one who had been such a disloyal friend to Him?"

That's what cauterized my bleeding wound—seeing that my son was not just a sufferer—but that he was first and foremost a sinner. The reality is that Jeff was not a loyal friend to Jesus, but even so, Jesus was a loyal Friend to him. That's the real story, not just for Jeff but for all of us.

Before, all I could see was Jeff's pain, but now I saw his sin and was devastated by the grace of God. Grace is something much more profound than God responding in sympathy to our suffering—it's all about Jesus, intentionally pouring Himself out in love for people who should rightfully have received just the opposite. I have a great predisposition to see only my own suffering, but in order to see grace I need a reality check. I have to see that sin is truly sin—and then I can see that grace is truly grace. When I see that sin is appalling then I can see that grace is amazing.

This clarifying of my perception had a wonderful bucking-up effect. The bleeding, weakening sympathy gave place to a little truth-produced backbone and courage. If good has come to me, to my son, to any of us, it's not because our suffering laid a rightful claim to it. Rachel is no suffering innocent and neither are her captive children. When I go to make a case for Jeff or for myself, the convincing arguments falter and peter out into silence. It's like raising the shades on a living room strewn with cigarette butts and spilled drinks the morning after. The daylight shines in and the evidence speaks for itself. This was no harmless party; this was dissolution.

I remember going into court with Jeff—straight out of a rehab family therapy meeting where his situation had been couched in no-fault terms of illness and need. The courtroom threw a whole different light on the situation. In there it was all a straightforward matter of culpability before the law. I could do nothing to protect him, I could put no compelling spin on his situation, and it came to me that this was the *true light*, this light of justice.

The reality is that we have no case before God. We threw our own selves away, flagrantly disregarding His right to our lives, and it is deadly serious business. Making excuses, defending ourselves, thinking we deserve a little slack—it all just makes matters worse for us. We have nothing left to do but hang our heads and wait for the gavel to come down and pronounce us guilty. When it comes down with a verdict of "forgiven," we can only look up and stare at the judge in amazement. When we realize this word has come to us by virtue of Jesus' death, our jaws just have to drop.

"Amazing Grace" has become a generic feel-good song that's lost it's punch. But this—this is truly amazing grace. This is mercy unsullied by any arguments that derive from us, from our good behavior or our neediness. This is the pure gorgeous mercy of God.

Jesus is God's amazing grace. He went outside the camp like the scapegoat bearing our sins; He became a *desechable* so that we could be brought home—and that "we" is not made up of a huddling mass of innocent children but of great, culpable sinners. Great good has come to us, and it's not because He owed us friendship, or anything else, but because He called us friends in spite of our faithless denials; He took on our guilt and laid down His life for us. He is our great Friend in court, the One who speaks on our behalf with an argument that satisfies every legal requirement.

All the glory, praise, and honor go to Him. It's really and truly not about us, it's not about Jeff; it's all about Jesus.

Finding Courage …
in their words:

Dear Charles and Janet,

When I first heard Jeff's name mentioned on the radio I thought, "I know who that is." I got out my school photo album with the classes and there was Jeff in a group of first graders I taught. Death has come to several of "my children" over the years since I taught them and a few at their own hands.

I know you must be so torn up over the "why" and your grief that he is gone from your life. I'm sure you have asked yourselves "What did we fail to do or understand that would have prevented this?"

I know you know our sovereign God and only He has the answer. It will probably be that you will never know fully, but He knows you and your heartache and will bring you His comfort. I hope that Jeff had been sensitive to the things of the Spirit and had trusted Jesus to be His Savior.

I pray that the Lord Jesus will minister His special comfort to you at this time.

Most sincerely in Christ,
Barbara

Dear Charles,

I feel so inadequate to say anything to you at this time. If I was near, I could just hug you and pray for you. But I'm so many miles away. Please know that we are praying for you and your family.

I've been thinking about the turmoil I felt when my dad died. My dad had a long slow death from emphysema and related problems. He got to the point where he would only want mom or me to care for him. I was going to college by then, and it was difficult, but his illness gave us some opportunity to work through some things between us after years of things not going well.

When he died, I felt such loss. Maybe it was grieving over all the stuff that we never really had as a father and a son that I wanted. Anyway, it seemed so final, and I felt so alone. People tried to make me feel better by saying that his illness was gone and he was whole. But inside I argued with myself about what God allowed. But then I realized that when God saw our sin, He died. The fact that Jesus died started to mean more to me than ever before. The loneliest thing for us, it seemed to me, is to die. We do it alone. I couldn't die with my dad.

But Jesus died with him. He died in his place. He was with my dad the whole way through everything in a way that He could not have been if it had not been for the cross and the tomb.

Charles, what I'm trying to say is that God died with my dad and He died with your son. His love is so much higher, so far beyond us. I hope that you all will be able to rest in the love that is far above and beyond and nearer than we can imagine.

Please know that I am thinking and praying for you a lot.

Will

Charles and Janet,

We had heard on your radio program just two days before about the passing of your son. We are grieved with you for this enormous loss. We both just groaned when we heard it.

It just means that his last act was to murder himself but according to Jesus' standard, I also have murdered. The blood of Jesus covers all.

At very hard times, we have sometimes found that we have been so lifted up by God that we felt we floated. It doesn't take away the pain, but it seems to be almost a divine anesthesia. I hope and pray that you would experience that.

Paul

~~~

Dear Charles and Janet:

Our hearts have been so saddened and burdened for you on receiving your letter last Tuesday telling us of Jeff's death. Yet even in our deep heartfelt love and burden for you precious friends, we have never sat where you have had to sit this week. But we do, day after day, continue keeping you at our precious Savior's breast, who understands and comforts with His perfect love and concern. How we wish that we could be with you these days.

One of our prayers on your behalf is that you will dwell on the good memories of Jeff's short time on this earth. We pray that the Lord will affix to your daily thoughts those memories that are beautiful, joyful, wholesome and loving, those moments when you know that Jesus was integrated into his life.

We love you and trust our Heavenly Father to fill this void in your lives with His undergirding strength and overshadowing love these days.

John and Betty

Finding Courage ...
in the Word:

ISAIAH 49:15–16

> *Can a mother forget the baby at her breast and have no compassion on the child she has borne? Though she may forget, I will not forget you!*
>
> *See, I have engraved you on the palms of my hands; your walls are ever before me.*

JOB 16:20–21

> *My intercessor is my friend as my eyes pour out tears to God;*
>
> *on behalf of a man he pleads with God as a man pleads for his friend.*

PSALM 41:9

> *Even my close friend, whom I trusted, he who shared my bread, has lifted up his heel against me.*

ZECHARIAH 13:6

> *If someone asks him, "What are these wounds on your body?" he will answer, "The wounds I was given at the house of my friends."*

MATTHEW 11:19

> *The Son of Man came eating and drinking, and they say, "Here is a glutton and a drunkard, a friend of tax collectors and 'sinners.'"*

MATTHEW 26:56

> *Then all the disciples deserted him and fled.*

JOHN 15:13–15

> *Greater love has no one than this, that he lay down his life for his friends.*

You are my friends if you do what I command.

I no longer call you servants, because a servant does not know his master's business. Instead, I have called you friends, for everything that I learned from my Father I have made known to you.

7

Finding
Courage ...

in a
hotel room

JESUS POURED OUT IMMENSE GRACE ON US. Even so, we were keeping something at bay; some threatening thought, prowling around at the edges of our minds, trying to get in. Whatever it was, we still didn't have the courage to go back home and take up life again, not yet, not until we processed and prayed a little more. Some vulnerability lingered in us that went beyond the grief.

Mike, one of the Oklahoma City friends, had come up to Charles in the cemetery after the funeral and announced, "I'm paying for you to stay a few nights in the Four Seasons hotel in Oklahoma City." Initially we weren't sure but now accepting his kind offer and recuperating seemed like the thing to do. Peter piled into the back of the minivan and went with Kate and Rich, and his little nieces on the long drive back to Washington, playing many games of "I spy" along the way.

"I spy something gray, Uncle Peter."

Countless guesses later, "I give up, Charlotte, what is it?"

"It's my imaginary elephant!"

Meanwhile we made the one-hour drive to Oklahoma City, checked in and crashed, hoping that the Lord's all-is-well would be strengthened in this retreat. Instead the dreaded thought finally broke through:

"Oh God, if only we'd done things differently…."

Jeff was dead. His life had come to a tragic end, and we were his parents, the ones responsible for his well-being. If only we'd understood, if only we'd known what to do. Maybe if I'd taken the psychiatrist more seriously who told me Jeff was clinically depressed when he was in fourth grade. Maybe if we hadn't sent him to that boot-camp rehab in Utah. Maybe we shouldn't have made him wear khakis to church.

If Charles had traveled less, if we hadn't moved so often, if we'd had a clear plan of what to do after he was kicked out of Christian school his junior year.

And then came the deeper regrets. If only Charles and he had shared more common interests, had better communication. If only I hadn't been so fearful all his life, so protective. If I'd had more courage, more confidence in God, maybe he would have had it too and learned to live with courage. Did my fears get communicated to him, my fears and unbelief?

The regrets terrified us—we wanted to cover our ears—but nothing would block them out. "This is laid at our door. We let this happen. And now there are no more opportunities to do it over, to make it better, to get it right."

Letters and e-mails come to Haven all the time from parents like us. One was a long letter from a mother whose son, Adam, was addicted to heroin. She described getting an emergency-room call after months of not knowing where he was and hearing a voice say, "Is this the family of Adam Rollins?" She rushed to his side and stayed there for two weeks while he recovered from a near fatal overdose and pneumonia. Finally the hospital released him and he promptly disappeared again into the world of needles and addiction. The letter was awash with sorrow, but one little line whispered more anguish than all the rest. It simply said: "I made mistakes."

"We made mistakes, Lord, and we're not even sure what they were."

Charles and I both came down with a stomach virus in that hotel room. The lovely expectations we'd had of ordering room service and pampering ourselves started vaporizing with the first ominous twinges. Soon we were wracked with heaving waves of nausea that wrung us out and left us weak. But they were nothing compared to the waves of regret. Wave after wave of sickening sorrowful responsibility for Jeff's death began breaking over our heads.

Moments in life come when you can't take one more step unless you have answers. You can't possibly move forward with that intense pain gripping your heart, any more than we could have run the mile doubled up with that stomach virus. You're left with no recourse but to cry out to the Lord, and if He doesn't answer, you will surely be lost, like one who goes down to the pit.

"Lord Jesus, we stand before You with deep regrets and great sorrow. What do we do with them?"

"Should we tell ourselves: 'We did the best we could. We couldn't have known. Hindsight is always 20/20. Others have done worse and their children turned out okay. We can't take responsibility for his decisions. Even if we could do it again, it probably wouldn't have made any difference'?"

"Should we recount all the things we thought we did right and say it wasn't our fault?"

All of these were possible answers with no doubt a grain of truth in them, and we gave each a turn, making a stab at reassuring each other and giving each other comfort, but they didn't heal our regrets; they didn't give us peace. We could do only one thing and that was to go to Jesus without making excuses, without any rationalizations and hear what He had to say.

"Lord, we've made mistakes. We can't defend our parenting record. We grieve for the ways we failed our son, for that matter, all three of our children. Lord, we're loaded down with sorrow."

It's not that we expected to hear an audible voice, but we did expect the Lord to communicate to us, and with that in mind, during a brief reprieve from his bathroom stints, Charles did a search in his laptop Bible software for the word "courage." Courage had become a sort of theme for us by then. Courage was what Cyndi and Lanning had driven miles to bring us and courage was the question on the bookmark under the sofa bed, Jeff's question, the one we needed to have answered for ourselves again and again:

"How can we find courage, for that is what we chiefly need?"

Frodo posed the question to the elf, Gildor, as he was standing in the woods outside the Shire looking for the wherewithal to go forward on his quest. Elves are like heavenly beings in Tolkien's tales, eternal keepers of deep wisdom, and as such, they are often frustratingly enigmatic when you need straight answers. Gildor told Frodo, "Courage is found in unlikely places," and poor Frodo had to make do with that.

Thankfully, Jesus is much more straightforward in what He says to us. From the moment we'd first heard about Jeff's death, He'd been directing us to the unexpected places and ministering courage to us when we got there. The deep healing we needed that day was in the very first courage reference Charles found and read aloud—Matthew 9—the story of the paralyzed man being lowered down in front of Jesus.

Jesus was in a house in Capernaum where crowds of people had pushed their way in to hear His words and receive His healing touch. The place was packed, but even so, the crowd made way for the Pharisees, the religious authorities, to enter in dignity and make their way to the front row where they could have a clear view of the proceedings. They usually showed up, not to be taught and not to be healed, but to check Jesus out and render a judgment about Him as a religious figure, or to ask Him trick questions.

Jesus healed one person after another but then something unusual happened. First a little dust started to trickle down from above His head, then a patch of light appeared on the floor in front of Him, pouring in from where a roof tile up above had been removed. Pretty soon a large opening in the roof appeared, and through it, slowly, a mat descended held by ropes, finally settling down on the floor at His feet. A paralyzed young man stretched out on it, gazing up at Jesus. Up above were his determined friends, peering through the hole they'd made in the roof, watching to see what Jesus would do. The Pharisees watched too.

The friends were full of faith in Jesus—we know that because it says, "Jesus saw their faith." As for the Pharisees, their operating assumption was: "We are blessed and privileged because we have done well. If you are suffering it is because you have sinned." The young man probably bought into that theory, as well. We know the disciples did because when another young man, blind from birth, was brought to Jesus, the disciples asked Him, "Who sinned, this man or his parents?" In other words: Who messed up here?

I can imagine how that paralyzed young man felt as he lay on his mat, powerless, exposed, and condemned. I think Jesus must have locked eyes with him and seen into his guilty conscience because the words He spoke were aimed right at that source of fear—words loaded with love and healing power. What He said was, "Take courage, son; your sins are forgiven" (Matt. 9:2 NASB).

Those are beautiful words and they speak directly to Frodo's question. Right away both of us identified ourselves with the friends who brought the young man to Jesus, and identified Jeff with the young man whose sins were forgiven. It all seemed to fit—the man's paralysis was a pretty good metaphor for Jeff's condition; we could see ourselves as being like the friends who were so determined to get him to Jesus for healing; the words of forgiveness Jesus spoke to him echoed the words I'd heard on the beach. The message coming through was that forgiveness is the up-front, most critical issue in life—Jesus obviously considered it this young man's number-one need and the greatest gift He could bestow on him. We found comfort in all of this because after all, the young man's ultimate well-being is what mattered, but still it didn't really touch on our regrets.

After a while the light slowly filtered in on us, and we finally realized that we were like that young man. Having a son like Jeff had brought on us the same sense of exposure to judgment he must have felt when all those eyes were on him. We were paralyzed on our mats when it came to Jeff—we'd been powerless to save him, and now we were immobilized by regret and condemnation and sorrow.

There's a subliminal message in all of us that echoes the

question the disciples asked Jesus, "Who sinned, this man or his parents?" The message says, "If your children grow up healthy, wealthy, and wise, you've done it right." The reverse message is there too, "If your children are messed up, it's because you've messed up." How our children turn out is the thing that either justifies us or condemns us as parents, as people. The remorse we felt about Jeff wasn't something we could just get up and dust ourselves off about and go on. We were paralyzed when it came to getting back into life, paralyzed by condemnation and sorrowful regrets. We just didn't have the heart for it. Where could we find the courage to keep moving ahead on our journey when Jeff's death was not just a great sorrow in our hearts but a finger pointing at us in accusation?

We hadn't found it trying to defend ourselves. Where we found it was in hearing the words Jesus spoke to that young man and hearing them as words spoken to us, applied to our sins.

"Take courage, your sins are forgiven."

Let me tell you, those are the sweetest words a guilty conscience loaded with regrets will ever hear. They got through to us because we'd been listening for an answer, expecting a word from the Lord, so when it came, our ears pricked up.

The words carried weight with us because we knew the identity of the One who spoke them. When Jesus pronounced the young man's sins forgiven, the Pharisees were all thinking, "That blasphemer—who is he to forgive sins? Only God can forgive sins." But He wasn't a blasphemer; He was exactly who the

Pharisees accused him of thinking He was, exactly who He claimed to be in forgiving the man's sins.

In that little house crammed with people, He alone had the authority to judge. One day all creation will be summoned to His court because Jesus is the Judge of the Living and the Dead, which means when He forgives sins, He has the absolute authority to actually do it. If He says condemnation has been removed—it has been removed—clean away. And it doesn't matter what anyone else thinks about it either because only His opinion matters.

When Jesus takes your sins away, it infuses you with the courage to stand up and walk back into life again. That's what Jesus told the young man to do—He demonstrated His authority to forgive sins by telling the young man to get up and by giving him the power to do it. When Jesus spoke, the young man rolled up his mat and walked out with a clear conscience, glorifying God.

Courage is impossible with an uneasy conscience. Guilty clamorings rattle you; your confidence is shaky, ready to give way to fear. Reassuring yourself that God's smile is on you may put the anxiety in the closet for a while, but it doesn't get rid of it; it's still there, waiting for a chance to pounce. But going undefended to Jesus and having His forgiveness reach all the way to your conscience simply drains the fear away. Courage comes because you have an answer for the Accuser. God has said, "No word spoken against you in accusation will stand. It is I who justifies you, who is he who condemns you?"

The Lord encouraged us to be bold and believe this—to believe He had wiped out the sorrowful scenario of failure and regret, and written another scenario, one where His love was resting on us, where our parenting was blessed by His grace, where He heard our prayers with great willingness to answer. Jesus was consumed by His zeal to vindicate us against our Accuser and bring us into His grace—consumed by death. Because of His death, our failure and powerlessness and all our sickening regrets were removed and replaced by His favor: "I have forgiven all your sins, and I am for you not against you."

"Who sinned, this man or his parents?"

The answer Jesus gave was, "Neither but this happened so that the works of God might be displayed in him."

Grace rewrites the scenario. Instead of the answer being, "They both sinned and they're both at fault and this is the mess their sins have made," He lays down His life so the answer can be, "No, this is an opportunity for My grace to blaze forth in all its glory."

What's it like to have Jesus speak forgiveness into your soul? It's like waking up from a nightmare on the first day of summer vacation. The final exam you were sweating over fades away as you emerge into the consciousness of a happy new morning. The promise of good things rushes in, and the undermining sense of dread evaporates along with all of your regrets.

It's like waking up with a hearty appetite after days of wrenching nausea. You open your eyes and see Jesus, the Lord of heaven and earth, standing there with a tray loaded with mouthwatering things to eat. The sickening sense of guilt and regret are gone, and instead there's the tray and the whole new death-bought day stretching out in front of you, full of savor. And best of all there's Jesus, His face brimming over with love and kindness and goodwill.

Finding Courage …
in their words:

Charles,

I know that you are probably being bombarded with e-mails these days, but I really wanted to let you know that you and your family have frequently been on my mind these days. There have been days where it has been hard to focus at times, because my heart is filled with sympathy for you.

Fifteen months ago, one of my best friends, who was a member of my Romania team, suddenly died of a seizure and passed on to be with our Lord. To this day I still think about Tim and miss him lots. I mention this because I have become friends with his parents and I watch as they struggle to live life without their eldest son. It has been very tough for them, but they continue to grow closer to the Lord and their family is strengthened as they bond together. They have hurt, but they have hope. I have seen their pain, and I can imagine yours. I feel deeply for you my friend!

Another great godly man once lost several sons, and I really like the way that he expressed

his anguish as he could not understand the
Lord's works:

> "Behold, I go forward but He is not there,
> And backward, but I cannot perceive Him;
>   When He acts on the left, I cannot behold Him;
>   He turns on the right, I cannot see Him.
>   But He knows the way I take;
>   When He has tried me, I shall come forth as gold.
>   (Job 23:8–10)

I am praying for you continually Charles.
Andrew

Dear Janet and Charles,

My deepest and sincerest condolences go out to you and your family with the passing of your son Jeff. Hanns had shared with me before your email arrived and prepared me but it still hit hard.

News of Jeff's passing came as a huge shock to us, but maybe not a total surprise. We are grateful that you trusted us and shared with us about this painful struggle in your family for all those years.

I forget exactly how long ago we were in Colorado together. Our oldest boys were just starting puberty. They were born only a few weeks apart. I remember you confided in me back then already that Jeff was troubled.

As you shared with me over the years I was humbled to witness your love and sacrifice. Blame God, blame Satan, blame the drugs and that culture, but please, do not ever blame yourself. I dont think I would have had the courage nor the pure energy to do everything you did to help Jeff.

I realize there is nothing I can say or do to comfort you now that Jeff is gone. I wish there was. I guess I can say but one thing: I too believe wholeheartedly that God exists and that He will reunite you and Jeff someday soon in a place free from sorrow. No doubt about it. I know that your faith comforts you, but it has to be good to know you are not alone in believing this.

You know our door is always wide open to you and I hope an opportunity will arise soon for us to get together.

With much love and sympathy, also from Marian,

Rinch

Dearest Charles and Janet,

We are praying for you as you rest and take a needed break from ministry. We also pray that the Lord will continue to minister to you in your grief. We are glad you are together and able to be away.

I was reading Ps. 106 today. It shows the compassion of the Savior even when we "sink into our sins, He looks on our distress and hears our cries and helps us because He remembers His covenant for our sakes." Amazing reassurance. What a beautiful Savior. I was encouraged at how He saves us in the presence of our captors. And he spreads a table for us in the presence of our enemies.

Love and miss you both so much. Can't wait to see you.

Love,

Linda & Ted

Mr. Morris,

I have always been so blessed by your daily programs and because I had been so busy at work, I had not listened for a week or so. So I was so saddened when, while listening yesterday, I learned that you and your wife had lost a son.

Please accept my deepest sympathy and know that my prayers are with you and your family. I am a single parent of a seventeen-year-old daughter. I feel like I made some major mistakes as a parent. But it is so wonderful that God's thoughts are not our thoughts, and His ways are not our ways. I am overwhelmed by His unceasing love for us in spite of ourselves. I pray that your family would feel His love and His peace during this difficult time.

God Bless! M.

Finding Courage ...
in the Word:

PSALM 23:5

> *You prepare a table before me in the presence of my enemies. You
> anoint my head with oil; my cup overflows.*

ISAIAH 49:25

> *But this is what the LORD says: "Yes, captives will be taken from war-
> riors, and plunder retrieved from the fierce; I will contend with those
> who contend with you, and your children I will save."*

ISAIAH 54:13

> *All your sons will be taught by the LORD, and great will be your
> children's peace.*

ISAIAH 65:23

> *They will not toil in vain or bear children doomed to misfortune; for
> they will be a people blessed by the LORD, they and their descendants
> with them.*

JEREMIAH 31:15–16

> *This is what the LORD says: "A voice is heard in Ramah, mourning
> and great weeping, Rachel weeping for her children and refusing to
> be comforted, because her children are no more."*
>
> *This is what the LORD says: "Restrain your voice from weeping and
> your eyes from tears, for your work will be rewarded," declares the
> LORD. "They will return from the land of the enemy."*

MATTHEW 9:2–7

Some men brought to him a paralytic, lying on a mat. When Jesus saw their faith, he said to the paralytic, "Take heart, son; your sins are forgiven."

At this, some of the teachers of the law said to themselves, "This fellow is blaspheming!"

Knowing their thoughts, Jesus said, "Why do you entertain evil thoughts in your hearts?

"Which is easier: to say, 'Your sins are forgiven,' or to say, 'Get up and walk'?

"But so that you may know that the Son of Man has authority on earth to forgive sins...." Then he said to the paralytic, "Get up, take your mat and go home."

And the man got up and went home.

8

Finding
Courage ...

down south

HEADING SOUTH FROM OKLAHOMA TO TEXAS in August is like going from the frying pan into the fire. We were doing it because we really wanted to go to church and hear Charles' friend, Dan Duncan, pastor at Believers Chapel in Dallas.

But was it hot. Dallas glares in the sun like a giant brass belt buckle, and Texans make no apology for the absence of shade. Physically we were still pretty iffy from the intestinal thing. As we drove into town, Charles thought maybe his stomach was ready for a banana split—which it wasn't. Still, we made it to the air-conditioned hotel room where we dropped our bags and stretched out on the bedspread with a groan. The groans continued off and on through the night, but Sunday morning found us sitting toward the front in Believers Chapel, weak but ready to take in something good.

This was our first public excursion since Jeff's death, and it was taking everything I had. I felt so conspicuous. I thought surely people must be seeing our sorrow-marked identity written all over us. A dear friend lost her twenty-two-year-old son a few months after Jeff, and she said for weeks she couldn't look in the mirror. She couldn't bear to have the anguished eyes of that grief-stricken mother looking back at her, forcing her to come face-to-face with her unwanted new self. In the old days people wore black, dressing themselves for the part, but the women got to hide their falling tears and puffy eyes behind a veil. I would have given a lot for a veil that morning.

Dan knew about Jeff, and we saw him take note of us in the congregation when he stood up to preach. Over the years every one of Charles' friends had heard about his heartbreak and fear for Jeff, about our search for solutions, and Dan along with many others, had prayed for him. That morning he happened to be preaching from Luke 9, on the story of the father who brought his demon-possessed boy to Jesus for healing.

For us, of course, he wasn't preaching about a remote incident several centuries removed. We were right there, identifying with every detail: the helplessness of the father who'd watched his son hurt again and again and not being able to protect him; the powerful hold of the Malevolent One, bent on destroying the boy; the father's desperate search for someone to help; the inability of the disciples to save the boy even though so many others had been delivered; the panic of the father when it seemed his son's was the one case that wasn't going to yield.

And then Jesus comes on the scene, down from the mountain where the wattage of His glory had blinded the disciples, down into the polluted valley where we live our broken lives, a man of sorrows acquainted with our grief.

Luke 9:37–38 (NASB) says, "A large crowd met him. And a man from the crowd shouted, saying 'Teacher, I beg you to look at my son.'"

The father goes on to summarize the boy's terrible condition for Jesus' benefit, telling him about the years of watching his son ravished by evil, and then adds the final hopeless note, "I begged your disciples to cast it out, but they could not."

What you get next is Jesus' strong adverse reaction to unbelief, "Oh perverted and faithless generation, how long must I be with you?" He was confronting a wall of unbelief—the unbelief of His disciples, the unbelief of the crowd, and the unbelief of the father—the whole group was intimidated and overwhelmed just like we have been so many times. This lack of faith profoundly grieved Jesus. They were respecting the enemy as the one with power rather than giving that respect to Him. Maybe some of them were just testing Jesus out to see what He could do. Even the disciples had been defeated.

The parallel passage in Mark's gospel has the father's unbelief coming through loud and clear in what he said next: "If You can do anything, take pity on us and help us." Jesus' response was, "If You can? Everything is possible for him who believes" (Mark 9:22–23).

One thing we know from our wrestling matches with God for Jeff is that a remark like this doesn't mean Jesus is throwing the responsibility back on us. Just the opposite. He's telling us to hand over the responsibility to Him. He's insisting we get a fix on Him, that we see who He is and get hold of the implications.

When the father cried out, "I do believe, help my unbelief," he was looking to Jesus to close the gap he couldn't close, to give him the faith he didn't have—and that was faith—just to cry out to Jesus for whatever he couldn't do, to provide whatever he lacked. If there's anything we'd learned by going down so far beyond all our resources, it's that you can cry out from any condition and Jesus will be there.

He's there and He tells you what he told the man, "Stop doubting and believe." And the very fact that this is what Jesus expects helps to take the doubt away. Believe! Stop doubting. Believe, because in Jesus there's every reason to believe.

Struggling in prayer for Jeff, we found that unbelief posed two basic questions that had to be answered. One is the question the man articulated: "If you can?" Does Jesus actually possess the ability to deliver the help we need? Those fears are noxious fumes that come wafting up out of hearts filled with the enormity of the problem. The anxiety-racked "ifs." But then there's Jesus—the Able One, the strong arm of God, who can command the enemy. All the power and authority have been given to Him; nothing can stand in His way because in His own body He has accomplished our redemption.

The Spirit opens our eyes to see the glory of the Lord, over and over again, and fills us up with *His* enormity. "If you can?" gives way to "Of course you can. You can do anything!" Doubt comes in because we can't imagine how it can happen. But we don't need to know the details; we just trust that He has the matter in hand. Again and again we've reached that same certainty at the end of desperate prayer.

The other question is the *willingness* question. Is Jesus *willing* to deliver the help we need? A leper came to Jesus once and spoke that question, "If you're willing, you can make me clean." Most translations say Jesus was "filled with compassion" when the man spoke to Him, but Today's New International Version says he was "indignant." When we were reading that version out loud to each other, that word jumped off the page. Why was Jesus indignant? Then we realized—He was indignant because the man doubted His compassion for his pain, His willingness to answer his request. It was as if the man's question hit right at the very heart of what Jesus' presence in the world is all about—He is here because He is willing. He went to the cross because He is willing. Willing is too weak of a word. His entire being is always, intentionally, passionately poured into helping us. And as the great master of understatement, Jesus told the man, "I am willing! Be clean." I am ashamed at how often His willingness is such a surprise to me. Haven't I seen His face? Hasn't He made Himself known to me again and again and confirmed in His words and in my experience that He is eager to hear and answer prayer?

Well, that Sunday, Dan's sermon got the willingness of Jesus across to us. We felt the rush of gladness as we caught a strong fresh glimpse of Jesus' face, forgiving us, overflowing with compassion toward the requests we bring to Him, insisting that we believe in Him.

What a huge relief for that father to give over the unsustainable responsibility and see Jesus handle it; to see Jesus enter into his desperate concern for his son and demonstrate both His deep compassion and His masterful authority. He delivered the boy from oppression with a command—but it wasn't without a struggle. The spirits convulsed him one last time, furiously reluctant to give him up, and then he lay there so still that everyone thought he was dead. But he wasn't. Jesus took him by the hand and gave him back to his father.

A friend later told Charles that Dan felt heartbroken seeing him out in the congregation since it hadn't turned out that way for him; since Jesus hadn't given him back his son. Charles was taken by surprise and said, "Oh, but I believe He has."

He may appear to be dead, but we believe the reality is that he's alive. We believe he's been delivered out of the relentless grip of the enemy just as surely as the boy Dan preached about, and someday, along with all the other joys of that day, the Lord will say, "Look, here's Jeff!" and there he'll be, forgiven, bright and beautiful, safe and sound, all new but still himself, our son. We believe the Lord has answered every prayer we ever prayed for Jeff, that Jesus has contended with our enemy and saved our son; that He is both able and willing to save to the uttermost, like the Bible says.

Do we wish we could see the deliverance with our own eyes here and now? Oh, yes. Isn't that what we expected Jesus to do? Yes, we expected it with all our hearts. Psalm 27:13 puts it into words, "Surely I believed I would see the goodness of the Lord in the land of the living."

The "land of the living" in the Bible means here on earth, not "wherever it is people go after death," and yes, of course we desperately wanted to see it happen in the land of the living, and yes, we believed we would. We know what Dan meant and we didn't want it to happen this way. We thought we were going to die when Jeff died. We would definitely have preferred to be telling a different story, one where we saw Jesus radically change his life. But Psalm 27:14 (NASB) has an answer. It says, "Wait for the Lord; be strong and let your heart take courage; yes, wait for the Lord."

No apologies, just "wait." What else can we do? We're waiting like never before. Our sights are set beyond the next year, beyond our own lives, onto a day that's set and coming— a great day, when the glory of Jesus will break through the pollution that blocks our view of reality. On that day we'll find ourselves on the mountain of the Lord and everything we

hoped for will be right before our eyes. Take courage and wait
for that day.

> The LORD of hosts will prepare
> a lavish banquet for all peoples
> on this mountain;
> A banquet of aged wine, choice
> pieces with marrow,
> And refined, aged wine.
> And on this mountain He will
> swallow up the covering which
> is over all peoples,
> Even the veil which is stretched
> over all nations.
> He will swallow up death for all
> time,
> And the Lord GOD will wipe
> tears away from all faces,
> And He will remove the
> reproach of His people from all
> the earth;
> For the LORD has spoken.
> And it will be said in that day,
> "Behold, this is our God for
> whom we have waited that He
> might save us.

This is the LORD for whom we
have waited;
Let us rejoice and be glad in
His salvation."
—Isaiah 25:6–9 (NASB)

On that day the party will finally begin. Whatever sorrow we have endured, however many tears we've shed, the Lord will wipe away every bit of it. It's a much bigger thing than merely seeing Jeff again. That day will be a day when the unveiled presence of Jesus will heal everything, even if from our present vantage point we can't see how that's possible. He will wipe our grief away. He is willing, He is able, and He will do it.

"Fix your eyes on the unseen things."

"But Lord, we can't see them."

"Yes, but fix your eyes on them. Give the mountain you cannot see the weight of ultimate reality. Don't buy into the present setup. Don't settle in like it's going to last forever. Make it a serious matter to get your life continually realigned with that day."

Having your hopes in this world dashed certainly moves that process along. Having the color drained away from the world forces you into a pilgrimage toward that recreated, redeemed world of living color that Jesus has accomplished for us. It etches the highway to Zion into your heart and shoves you out the door onto the road home. Jeff's death certainly had that effect on us. The beauty of Jesus had been enhanced in our eyes. The price He paid had become more breathtaking, more central. We were adhering to Him like Velcro because of our pain and weakness, and our future expectations had been riveted to the day of His return.

The smog in the valley can be so thick sometimes that you can't see your hand in front of your face. But then the joy comes again like a shaft of light from the mountaintop, and you turn your face toward it and start walking home again.

Finding Courage ...
in their words:

Dear Mr Morris,

I am so sad to hear the news of your son's death.
But know this: The tormentor that made his life a
nightmare will never torment him again. I

~~~

Dear Charles and Janet,

Just a note to let you know that many of us are
praying for you and your family. May Christ thru
the work of the Holy Spirit embrace you with His
love as you rest in His Majesty, Sovereignty, and
Grace.

Lanning and Cyndi shared with us last Sunday
night about their time with you. Lanning shared
out of Romans 1 on the topic of "encouragement."
Remember that encouragement really means—"passing
on courage." So may you sense the power of the Lord
passing on HIS courage to you and your family.

Take care.

KL

~~~

Mr. Morris,

The story of your son rocked me, brother. You are in my prayers.

I'm 30 years old, and I must share with you that I was walking around in the shoes of a dead man. While I'm still euphoric with my reconnection with God, I still see the reflection of this dead man in my parents' and sister's eyes when they look at me. They worry that I will return to the despair that I felt for so many years. Even in this short time, I see that awful reflection fading, as God has been so gracious with opportunities for me to show them that I'm actually alive and well.

Your story rocked me so hard, and my heart hurts so much for you because from what you've described, your son and I had so much in common. I drank, drugged, did anything to feel any relief from the hopelessness. I attempted to take my life. I ended up in hospitals, you name it.

My friend, looking back over the past 14 years, I would take any hell over the feeling of separation and alienation I experienced having chosen to live without God in my life.

I wept and wept when God flooded into my heart. I was so ashamed of not only what I had done, but I blamed God for not giving me faith, if there

was a God in the first place. I presented this problem to a Christian and he practically dared me to
ask God for faith. That was something I had never
done, and despite the simplicity of doing it, I
would not do it. But ... PRAISE HIM ... I finally
did. I almost did it sarcastically ... as if I was dar-
ing God Himself to give some nobody like me faith
that He's there and that He cares.

Well, the joke was on me!! No lights, no smoke, no
fireworks ... but the next day I woke up and things
were different, and they haven't been the same since.

I can't tell you how badly I hope you read this.
Mr. Morris, Jeff is with God now. Jeff suffered
plenty right here on earth. The God who swept
through the tiny crack in the door to my heart
LOVES us and weeps for us when we feel pain. The
Bible says this. I asked for faith in a half-hearted,
bordering-on-insulting way, and God received this
crumpled invitation and brought me home.

I can't imagine going back. It's horrifying. I will
pray for you Mr. Morris. The grief in your voice
hurts my heart.

With much love and many prayers,

S.

Finding Courage …
in the Word:

PSALM 84:5–7

Blessed are those whose strength is in you, who have set their hearts on pilgrimage.

As they pass through the Valley of Baca, they make it a place of springs; the autumn rains also cover it with pools.

They go from strength to strength, till each appears before God in Zion.

ROMANS 8:22–25

We know that the whole creation has been groaning as in the pains of childbirth right up to the present time.

Not only so, but we ourselves, who have the firstfruits of the Spirit, groan inwardly as we wait eagerly for our adoption as sons, the redemption of our bodies.

For in this hope we were saved. But hope that is seen is no hope at all. Who hopes for what he already has?

But if we hope for what we do not yet have, we wait for it patiently.

2 CORINTHIANS 4:16–18

Therefore we do not lose heart. Though outwardly we are wasting away, yet inwardly we are being renewed day by day.

For our light and momentary troubles are achieving for us an eternal glory that far outweighs them all.

So we fix our eyes not on what is seen, but on what is unseen. For what is seen is temporary, but what is unseen is eternal.

REVELATION 21:1-5

Then I saw a new heaven and a new earth, for the first heaven and the first earth had passed away, and there was no longer any sea.

I saw the Holy City, the new Jerusalem, coming down out of heaven from God, prepared as a bride beautifully dressed for her husband.

And I heard a loud voice from the throne saying, "Now the dwelling of God is with men, and he will live with them. They will be his people, and God himself will be with them and be their God.

"He will wipe every tear from their eyes. There will be no more death or mourning or crying or pain, for the old order of things has passed away."

He who was seated on the throne said, "I am making everything new!"

9

Finding
Courage ...

to go ON

YEARS AGO MY LITTLE GRAY AND WHITE CAT, Lucy, brought
me a special gift in the wee morning hours and primly laid it on the
pillow beside me. I opened my eyes and there it was—a dead rat. Fear
is like that dead rat. You go to sleep full of faith and in the morning
you wake up and fear is staring you in the face and you're crying out
again, "Where can I find courage? That is what I chiefly need!"

We woke up the day of our scheduled return to normal life,
and that big, dead rat was lying on the pillow. We were supposed
to drive to Oklahoma City, get on a plane, and wing it back to
California but we just couldn't. We couldn't muster up the heart
for it. We simply didn't have the wherewithal.

Back home hard things were waiting—the hardest being a
layoff of staff at Haven because of financial shortages. It was like

cutting off an arm or a leg to lose those people—grief on top of grief—and it was weighing heavy on Charles. There was the responsibility to do the daily program, which, from where we were standing, looked like the sheer face of a cliff, impossible to scale. There was Peter. We had a foreboding that we'd barely begun to plumb the depths of our own grief, but what about his? How could we go forward when the wind had been taken flat out of our sails?

"Lord, could we go straight from Dallas to the wedding feast of the Lamb?"

No, we were still in Dallas with our suitcases opened on the unmade bed, trying to get it together to make the plane while the shadows were lying heavy on our hearts. Charles suggested we just stop packing and pray. It was a Psalm 143 sort of prayer, "Answer us quickly, O Lord, our spirits fail. Do not hide your face from us or we will become like those who go down to the pit. Let us hear your lovingkindness in the morning for we trust in you. Let your good Spirit lead us on level ground. Revive us. Bring our souls out of trouble."

And then into our darkness, like a light slowly dawning, once again the Spirit brought the thought of Jesus. We had forgotten the nearness of the Lord and He reminded us of it. "We have Jesus." It was music carried on the wind; it was water poured on our parched souls. He was there, He was answering us, He loved us, and we weren't going to have to do this alone. We both sensed the same lightening of our hearts—and we made it—to the airport, on to the plane, buckled in, flying home.

After takeoff Charles asked me, "How long has it been since the call came from Suzanne? It seems like light years, another life. Remember the night after he died? We were sitting in the living room with Ted and Linda. Can that have been just over two weeks ago?"

I remembered. Ted, our pastor, and his wife, my friend of the never-ending waves of grace, were hanging in there with us even though it was one in the morning and he had to preach the next day. The clock was ticking, we were exhausted, but we weren't quite ready to say, "You guys go home; we're okay." Sitting together, warming our hands around our coffee cups, was easing us into saying "good night" to the day our son had died.

"Do you remember what you said, Chas? 'For all his problems, we believe Jeff had a true faith in Jesus.' And Ted said, 'Well, there you go then. It's all about Jesus.'"

It's all about Jesus. There you go. Those words had given us courage when Ted said them a lifetime ago, back when Jeff's death was still too new to grasp. Now that same reality was the single thing giving us courage to face plunging back into the fray again two weeks later. Talking together on the plane, we both agreed there was only one future we could contemplate with courage—and that was one where the days ahead were all about Jesus—where He was both our reason and our strength to live.

I'm not sure that's an altogether bad state to be in.

Life has a way of spinning us in tighter and tighter circles around unimportant things, orbiting around the all-consuming things that don't really matter. It's very hard looking after our own little universe, trying to pull good things in, struggling to keep everything in its place. A violent breaking up of our world can get us orbiting around Christ instead of ourselves.

Great weakness and a complete absence of internal resources leave you with nowhere else to go. Instead of spinning unanchored out in space, you go to Him and He becomes the big thing, the thing that holds you fast. But in a weird way, that leaves you at liberty—to fling yourself wholesale into Him—to make life a freewheeling orbit around Him—to let go and lean hard into Him and be kept in His orbit by His strength alone. Charles and I both felt we'd been yanked out of normal life and left with only one life we could live—a life where we were either orbiting around Him, or completely out of control.

The Sunday before, when we'd felt all that thanksgiving, all that pure and simple gladness from seeing Him clearly—we'd had a sort of cavalier attitude. Who cares what happens from here on out? Let's inventory our assets and only count Jesus because He's the only thing worth having. We belong to Him, our sins are forgiven, His love is our armor, and He's coming again—so let's hurtle ourselves headlong into giving Him glory. We had reasons to live: We could delight in His presence; we could devote ourselves to His people; we could invest in His ventures.

This day, when a great weakness of spirit had come upon us, we were cast back on Jesus yet again. But any way you cut it, we had no way of going back to normal life. We had no way to contemplate doing life at all—except by contemplating Jesus. That day, we were fragile, totally overcome, grief-debilitated people, with no choice but to return to a demanding situation, and yet knowing we were completely devoid of the resources to do it. So we had to turn that all over to Jesus and let Him carry us—like a sack of potatoes. As we taxied into LAX, we armed ourselves with the fact that there was no more condemnation left for us and that Jesus was for us, not against us. Facing the impossible was going to be possible because we weren't going to have to do it—He was going to do it.

And He has. Again and again.

I'm writing this a year later, and I can tell you that He has. I remember the October afternoon after Jeff's death when I walked out to pick up the mail. Pulling our stack out of the box, I saw right on top an official looking envelope from the coroner's office. Three months after the fact, here at last was the final determination of the cause of Jeff's death. Inside the house I dropped everything, opened it slowly, and just stared at the heading, "Certificate of Death." Down a little farther under "cause of death," it said "accidental" with an explanation, "overdose of amphetamines and methamphetamines."

So there it was in black and white. Jeff was officially dead. Who could argue with such a formal-looking document? I felt like someone was mocking the very idea of his rescue, his redemption, his life enduring beyond death.

"Fool. There's no glad ultimate ending to this story. This is reality. Death has had the last word. It was just a huge tragic mistake. A defeat. A great waste. What a joke to think there's any more to it than that."

I gave way to the pain of that piece of paper. Jeff. Our beautiful, beautiful boy. "Oh God, I love him so much."

We have a picture of him at about ten years of age, going up the gangplank onto a cruise ship we took on a three-day trip into the Caribbean. He's looking down at the camera as he mounts the metal gangway, backpack on his back, so full of happiness, his face shining in the sunshine. "Lord, we loved him so much and oh … all that energy we poured into saving him, protecting him, trying with all our might to secure his well-being. What is the truth? Have You stepped in and redeemed him? Have You rewritten this script?"

I haven't yet come close to reaching the limits of the pain of losing Jeff. It's like falling and falling and when you finally resurface and leave off grieving for a while, you know you still haven't come near to the touching bottom.

I prayed that day in October—with desperation—and I will tell you what came to me as an answer, with all the healing freshness of light pouring into my darkness. I thought of Abraham, going up the mountain with Isaac tripping along beside him, happy about the outing, all-unknowing about the sentence hanging over him. He was walking toward death, and Abraham walking beside him could not save him. His son trusted him to make everything okay, and he knew he was powerless to do it. And yet, when Isaac asked him, "Father, where is the sacrifice?" Abraham didn't say, "You are the sacrifice, Isaac." He said, "God will provide."

God will provide the sacrifice.

And the son will be saved.

Isaac's death was mocking the joy of that day, like the death certificate mocked that picture of Jeff going up the gangway. But at the top of the mountain, caught in the bushes was a ram, a sacrifice, provided by God to take Isaac's place. God had rewritten the script—life for Isaac, death for the ram. When Abraham came down again, after sacrificing the ram, he named the mountain, "God will provide."

And then I thought about Sarah, Isaac's mother, straining for that first sight of them. Did she know what God had told Abraham to do? Did she share her husband's faith in God? I imagine her waiting and watching to see if Abraham would come back alone. She would have seen Abraham first—he would have been taller. And then, to her great joy, lo and behold, she would have seen Isaac, alive, walking along beside his father, coming home.

So I looked at that piece of paper, that certificate of death, and I answered it, right out loud, "Yes, but God has provided a sacrifice. Death isn't the last word, it's only the second to last word. The last word is 'Life.'"

Finding Courage …
in their words:

Charles and Janet,

Davileen and I were grieved to hear the report of your son's death. Words cannot express how we feel and how we wish we could be close by to encourage in some way. We know that Jeff was dear to you. Davileen remarked how she and Janet spoke about Jeff at Brittany's reception. And that reminded us of our first discussion about him with you all in our dining room in Miami so many years ago. Thank you for sharing about Jeff's trust in his Savior; I know that comforts your hearts.

In times of doubt and disquiet I have found the first question and answer of the Heidelberg Catechism to be a source of assurance.

What is your only comfort in life and death?

That I, with body and soul, both in life and death, am not my own, but belong unto my faithful Savior Jesus Christ; who with His precious blood has fully satisfied for all my sins, and delivered me from all the power of the devil; and so preserves me that without the will of my heavenly Father not a hair can fall from my head; yea, that all things must be subservient to my salvation, wherefore by His Holy Spirit He also assures me of eternal life, and makes me heartily willing and ready, henceforth, to live unto Him.

May the Lord sustain you in these days and grant you a very special sense of His presence.

We love you,

Dominic and Davileen

Dear Charles,

I dont know you personally, but in Christ you are known. I couldnt help but respond by an e-mail when I heard of your grief. Peace be with you.

As you have comforted others, may the peace of Christ also comfort you.

Some time ago, I was not having the best of days, in fact, I was having a terrible day. A patient I had operated on wasnt doing so well and had to be taken back to surgery. I was worried. It just so happened that I turned on the radio and there was "Haven Today" with Charles Morris speaking on antidepressants vs sugar pills. It was a wonderful message for me. You spoke of

Jonathan Edwards and three points from a sermon
he gave many years ago:

1. All that appears bad will become good.
2. All that is good won't be taken away.
3. The best is yet to come.

I was greatly encouraged by your message. May
the comfort and peace that you bring others be the
comfort & peace that sustains you now, in Christ.
Your Brother in the Lord,
Sidney

Hello Charles,
I am a regular listener of your program and I
want you to know how deeply sorry my wife and I
feel for your loss. We are praying that God will
carry you and your family through this challenge
and of course we know He will.
I was at a retreat last weekend and heard many
testimonies about how God had healed loved ones of
cancer and heart disease, etc, in answer to prayer.
And, we know that God is still in the healing
business, so the truth of these testimonies is real to
those who know the Lord.

A friend of mine turned to me and commented on how wonderful still it would be to hear a testimony about how someone had prayed for healing, and their loved one died, but God is still God. Not 5 minutes later, we heard such a testimony. In your loss you have resoundingly said that God is still God, and all of what happens to us in this life is part of His magnificent plan for our eternal lives. You ministered to my heart and so many others last week and this morning, as Haven Ministries constantly leads us to the Foot of the Cross where Jesus paid it all ... for us.

God Bless you.

Neil

Finding Courage ...
in the Word:

PSALM 73:28

> But as for me, it is good to be near God. I have made the Sovereign
> LORD my refuge; I will tell of all your deeds.

JOHN 14:15–18

> If you love me, you will obey what I command.
>
> And I will ask the Father, and he will give you another Counselor
> to be with you forever—the Spirit of truth. The world cannot accept
> him, because it neither sees him nor knows him. But you know him,
> for he lives with you and will be in you.
>
> I will not leave you as orphans; I will come to you.

2 CORINTHIANS 5:14–15

> For Christ's love compels us, because we are convinced that one died
> for all, and therefore all died. And he died for all, that those who
> live should no longer live for themselves but for him who died for
> them and was raised again.

2 CORINTHIANS 12:9–10

> But he said to me, "My grace is sufficient for you, for my power is
> made perfect in weakness." Therefore I will boast all the more gladly
> about my weaknesses, so that Christ's power may rest on me.
>
> That is why, for Christ's sake, I delight in weaknesses, in insults, in
> hardships, in persecutions, in difficulties. For when I am weak, then I
> am strong.

GENESIS 22:14

*So Abraham called that place The L*ORD *Will Provide. And to this day it is said, "On the mountain of the L*ORD *it will be provided."*

Before You Close This Book

COURAGE ALWAYS COMES TO US BY STRANGE, painful ways. It's never a smooth, easy process. John Bunyan wrote, "It is wounding work, this breaking of the hearts; but without wounding there is no saving.... Where there is grafting there is a cutting. The graft must be let in with a wound; to stick it onto the outside of the tree bark or to tie it on with a string would be of no use. Heart must be set to heart and back to back or there will be no sap from root to branch. And this, I say, must be done by a wound."

The courage you just read on the previous pages came through an intense wounding in the hearts of my friends Charles and Janet Morris, like a vinedresser hammering a graft deep into the damp inner pulp of a tree. God was after much more than their nodding agreement that, yes, Christ was their Savior; much more than names in His book and hands to His plow—He was after their hearts and souls, bud, branch, blossom, rain, sun, and soil. *Everything.*

When people experience that kind of ragged-edge pain, when they come out the other side a little breathless and dazed, they do not—they simply cannot—sit down with pen in hand and relay object lessons for the rest of us. A story like theirs is not about takeaway value. As Charles and Janet told me, "We just wanted to capture and tell the raw reality of our pain and how it brought us face-to-face with the raw reality of what Jesus has done for us and for our son." Sounds like a grafting to me. And as I've come to understand in my own pain as a quadriplegic of forty years, God grafts those He loves.

Then again, this story of profound courage does have something we can take away. Charles and Janet "set heart to heart" by taking us deeper into the fellowship of sharing in Christ's sufferings. And there, in the secret inner sanctum of that fellowship, they help us glimpse the source of all courage—the painfully beautiful, raw, and tender reality of our suffering Savior. He bore our hell so that one day we might have heaven. This book helped me see Jesus in that light. And *that's* what gives courage.

In fact, before you close this book and move on, listen to Janet describe that reality one more time:

"Life has a way of spinning us in tighter and tighter circles around unimportant things, orbiting around the all-consuming things that don't really matter. It's very hard looking after our own little universe, trying to pull good things in, struggling to keep everything in its place. A violent breaking up of our world can get us orbiting around Christ instead of ourselves.

"Great weakness and a complete absence of internal resources leave you with nowhere else to go. Instead of spinning unanchored out in space, you go to Him and He becomes the big thing, the thing that holds you fast. But in a weird way, that leaves you at liberty—to fling yourself wholesale into Him—to make life a freewheeling orbit

around Him—to let go and
lean hard into Him and be
kept in His orbit by His
strength alone."

Or this little glimpse:

"No apologies, just 'wait.' What
else can we do? We're waiting
like never before. Our sights are
set beyond the next year,
beyond our own lives, onto a
day that's set and coming—a
great day, when the glory of
Jesus will break through the
pollution that blocks our view
of reality. On that day we'll find
ourselves on the mountain of
the Lord, and everything we
hoped for will be right before
our eyes. Take courage and wait
for that day."

I'm sure Janet and Charles would give anything to have
their son back. I'd love to have back the use of my arms and
legs. Really. But like my friends, I'll settle for the courage to
face life as it is. After all, the pain has set me heart to heart

with my precious Lord ... and a wounding like that is what makes life a freewheeling dance of joy.

And you don't have to lose your son, or break your neck, to believe it.

—Joni Eareckson Tada,
The Joni and Friends International Disability Center

RESOURCES

Sometimes finding home isn't always a direct path.

Jim Daly, president and CEO of Focus on the Family, managed to rise above his harrowing childhood that began in the Compton suburb of Los Angeles. In this deeply personal memoir, he relives being orphaned at an early age, moving from house to house, through the doors of twenty-three temporary homes and the care of countless adults whose intentions were not always in Jim's best interest, to the pivotal moment when he encountered Christ and surrendered to His care. Shifting his focus from his hellish situation to God's

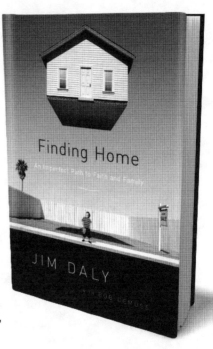

Hardcover with Jacket, 232 pages, 6" x 9"
ISBN: 978-0-7814-4533-7
$22.99

redeeming grace, Jim began the improbable journey to become the head of one of the most powerful and influential Christian organizations in the world. Let Jim's life story affirm that God can transform heartbreak into hope and triumph.